The Congo in Flemish Literature

THE CONGO IN FLEMISH LITERATURE

An Anthology of Flemish Prose
on the Congo, 1870s–1990s

Edited by Luc Renders and Jeroen Dewulf

Leuven University Press

© 2020 by Leuven University Press / Presses Universitaires de Louvain / Universitaire Pers Leuven Minderbroedersstraat 4, B-3000 Leuven (Belgium)
All rights reserved. Except in those cases expressly determined by law, no part of this publication may be multiplied, saved in an automated data file or made public in any way whatsoever without the express prior written consent of the publishers.

Every effort has been made to contact all holders of the copyright to the extracts of Flemish prose contained in this publication. Any copyright holders who believe that extracts have been translated without their knowledge are asked to contact the publisher.

ISBN 978 94 6270 217 2
e-ISBN 978 94 6166 336 8
D/2020/1869/28
NUR: 621
https://doi.org/10.11116/9789461663368

Translation: Grady Tarplee, with the assistance of L. DuLac
Layout: Coco Bookmedia
Cover design: Daniel Benneworth-Gray
Cover illustration: Kuba textile. Museum Afro Brasil / CC BY-SA (https://creativecommons.org/licenses/by-sa/4.0)

Table of Contents

PART 1
THE CONGO IN FLEMISH LITERATURE 9
   1. Flemish Literature 11
   2. The Colonial Era 13
   3. The Postcolonial Period 23
   4. Conclusion 27

PART 2
SELECTED EXTRACTS OF FLEMISH PROSE 29

Aldemar-Camille van der Cruyssen 31
   A Peaceful Crusade

Cyriel Buysse 35
   White Depravity

Pieter Danco 41
   A Mini-Europe in the Tropics

Pieter de Mey 47
   A Giant Step for Civilization

Constant De Deken 53
   A Missionary with a Cause

Henri van Booven 59
   No Place for Europeans

Henri Bossaerts 67
   White Injustice

Leo Bittremieux   77
    Light in the Darkness

Ernest Tilemans   81
    True Interracial Love

René Poortmans   85
    Under the Leaden Sun

Jean Gustave Schoup   91
    A Tragic Fate

Adolf Verreet   95
    Paternalistic Benevolence

Bert Nacht   103
    No Place like Home

Alfons Walschap   111
    Inner Conflict

Gerard Walschap   117
    A Humane Approach to Colonization

Jac. Bergeyck   127
    From a Congolese Perspective

Piet van Aken   135
    Cynical Power Struggles

Jan van den Weghe   143
    A Plea for Cooperation

Robrecht De Sadeleer 151
    The Disillusionment of the Colonial

Daisy Ver Boven 155
    Friendship between Black and White

Jef Geeraerts 163
    Paradise Lost

Paul Brondeel 169
    The Agony of a Nobody

Lieve Joris 175
    In Search of the Real Congo

Marcus Leroy 183
    Political Games

List of References **189**

PART 1
THE CONGO IN FLEMISH LITERATURE

1. Flemish Literature

This publication is the first anthology of Flemish prose on the Congo, the former colony of Belgium, in English translation. Flemish literature on the Congo has traditionally been neglected in international scholarship. This restricted perspective is all the more regrettable in light of the fact that the large majority of Belgians who went to work in the African colony came from Flanders.

Flanders is a term used to refer to the northern part of Belgium, where Dutch is the standard language for official and written communication. Thus, Flemish authors essentially write in the same standard language as their Dutch counterparts in the Netherlands. Readers interested in how the Congo and the Congolese were perceived by Belgian authors should take the important differences between French- and Dutch-speaking regions in Belgium into consideration. Unlike the heavily industrialized francophone south of Belgium, around the time of Belgian independence in 1830 Flanders was a predominantly rural and underdeveloped area. The poverty of Flanders in that epoch explains why French, the native language of Belgians in the south, was adopted as the country's only official language when it gained its independence. Ever since, Belgium has had a history of disputes between the two linguistic communities, out of which the speakers of Dutch have gradually managed to attain equal language rights. The social, cultural, and linguistic differences between the north and south are reflected in Belgian literature. While French literature in Belgium has traditionally followed a Parisian model that is profoundly influenced by liberalism and socialism, Flemish literature has tended to be characterized by a deeply Catholic, morally conservative, and parochial worldview. Flemish authors have often displayed a tendency to write from the position of the oppressed and to use literature as a means to express grievances against the country's French-speaking elite.

The same dichotomy between authors using Dutch and those using French applies to Belgian colonial literature about the Congo. Despite the fact that most Belgians who lived in the Congo came from Flanders, the only de facto official language in the colony was French. At the same time, while Flemish colonials in the Congo would also occasionally write literature in French, they mostly did so in their Dutch mother tongue. These literary works were usually published in Flanders and exclusively targeted the domestic market.

2. The Colonial Era

To Colonize in Order to Civilize

Belgium's colonial history began with King Leopold II (1835–1909). After a number of failed attempts to acquire a colony in the Far East, Leopold shifted his focus to Africa. The organization of an international geographical conference in Brussels in 1876 provided a cover for his imperialistic ambitions. The topics for discussion at the gathering were "the suppression of the slave trade in Central Africa, the gathering of further scientific knowledge about the area, and the bringing of civilization to the peoples living there."[1] The conference decided to set up the International Africa Association, split up into a number of national committees.

The Belgian National Committee became the vehicle for Leopold's colonial campaign. In 1878, the king engaged Henry Morton Stanley (1841-1904) to establish a number of settlements along the Congo River. In the context of the Conference of Berlin in 1884–1885, at which European colonizing nations signed agreements regarding each other's rights and obligations in Africa, the Congo landed in Leopold's lap as his private property. The colonization of this overseas territory began immediately. After the inhumane treatment of the Congolese population was revealed in an official report drafted by the British Consul in the Congo Roger Casement (1864–1916) and through the sustained campaign of British activist Edmund Dene Morel (1873–1924), Leopold had to give up control over his kingdom on the equator. He passed the colony on to the Belgian state in 1908.

Parliament was initially hesitant to assume this responsibility but eventually conceded under pressure from the country's economic elite, who were eager to exploit the Congo's natural resources, as well as the leaders of the Catholic Church in Belgium, who had ambitions to transform the territory into a Catholic stronghold. Under the pretext of bringing Western

---

1   Foeken, D. *"België behoeft een kolonie"*. *De ontstaansgeschiedenis van Kongo Vrijstaat* (Antwerp/Amsterdam: De Vries en Brouwers, 1985), 19–20.

civilization to the Congo and of demonstrating Belgium's position as a model colonial power, the exploitation of the Congo continued but without the brutal excesses that had characterized King Leopold's reign of terror. The Belgian state, church, and industry cooperated in the exploitation and Christianization of the Congo, a process that extended well into the 1950s.

The 1958 World Exhibition in Brussels provided Belgium with an opportunity to demonstrate its colonial ambitions to the world. Colonial enthusiasm was aroused through the Congolese pavilion, where an indigenous village was erected and colonial achievements were highlighted. The exhibition also welcomed some six hundred Congolese guests. Amongst them were the future leaders of the Congolese Republic, Patrice Lumumba (1925–1961) and Joseph-Désiré Mobutu (1930–1997). In Brussels, they and other African intellectuals were treated in the same way as Europeans for the first time. The mutual contacts between the young Congolese elite provided a strong impetus for the yearning for independence. What had been intended as a celebration of Belgian colonialism ended up being the inception of Congo's independence.

Colonial Ethos

Like other Europeans in Africa during the colonial era, Flemish colonials strongly believed in the superiority of Western civilization and in the duty of Europeans to bring civilization to the "dark continent." Most of the texts written by Flemish authors who (had) lived in the colony were characterized by a conviction that they were contributing to a great and noble cause. An example is the following quote from Sylva De Jonghe's essay *Het koloniale in de literatuur* (The Colonial in Literature, 1938):

> The colonial is everything related to the colony, to the profit region, which is exploited by a more advanced and more civilized country, in order to civilize the colony and to uplift the population. Indeed, civilization seems to be the first objective of colonization. Civilizing means the creation of a

new and better social environment and the spreading of the greatest of all benefactions: spirituality and Christianity.[2]

This type of convoluted and contradictory reasoning, riddled with inconsistencies and misrepresentations, is typical of a large number of literary texts by Flemish colonials. In spite of the fact that Leopold II was forced to hand over his private property to the Belgian state after the disclosure of a catalogue of horrors, many of these writers seemed to be suffering from collective amnesia regarding this unsavory episode in their country's past. Significantly, A.-C. Van der Cruyssen concluded his description of the Congo in *Afrika, naar de beste bronnen* (1877; Africa on the Basis of the Best Sources) with the following climactic exhortation: "Yes, it will become a general crusade, no longer with the sword in hand but with words of peace and conviction, with feelings of love in the heart, with self-sacrifice in the soul!"[3]

This song of praise for the mammoth civilizing task sounds uninterrupted and vociferous throughout the entire colonial period. An example is Pieter Danco's heroic description of the building of the railway line between Boma and Stanley Pool in *Ook een ideaal* (1896; Also an Ideal), the first Flemish novel about the Congo. When the African railway workers revolt against their treatment and launch an attack on their white bosses, Danco describes them as raging animals, who are crushed with no regard for life or limb. This assault is no more than a minor incident that momentarily enlivens the plot but is quickly forgotten. However, it clearly delineates the civilizing mission. In the colony, the power of the colonizers is absolute; any perceived threat from the Africans is met with maximum force.

The Congo was to a large degree a segregated society; for many colonials, the only Africans they really got to know were their servants, whom they called "boys." As French was the de facto official language in the colony, the Flemish communicated with their servants in a language that was foreign to them and used Dutch among themselves, a language the Congolese could not understand. Dutch, therefore, acquired a bad reputation among

---

[2] De Jonghe, S. *Het koloniale in de literatuur* (Turnhout: Van Mierlo-Proost, 1938), 7.

[3] Van der Cruyssen, A.-C. *Afrika, naar de beste bronnen* (Courtrai: Ch. Vandesteene, 1877), 144.

some Congolese, who perceived it as a language used to keep things secret. Moreover, some Flemish people living in the Congo were of humble origin and had no experience whatsoever in dealing with servants. The sudden increase in social status upon arrival in the colony posed a challenge that could sometimes lead to conflicts and tensions. While Flemish women often felt disoriented in an environment where all traditionally female tasks were performed by the "boys", men frequently had difficulties accepting that their wives spent most of the day surrounded by male servants. Although a strong emotional connection could sometimes develop between Flemish colonials and certain servants, this relationship was often characterized by recurrent misunderstandings, miscommunication, and mistrust. Finally, their perceived rise in social status also had a detrimental impact on the reputation of colonials in the motherland. The constant references to the "boys" in the stories they brought home from Africa during their extended holidays often aroused jealousy from family members in Flanders. Not surprisingly, literature written from the perspective of Flemish colonials displays a conviction that people at home were unable to grasp the true magnitude of the colonial endeavor. This difference in perception may also explain the cold domestic reception of repatriates after Congo's independence and the widespread feeling in Flemish society that, in losing everything they had built up in the colony, repatriates got what they deserved.

Flemish Nationalism

Flemish identity grew out of a shared feeling of being discriminated against in a nation where the French-speaking upper class was once in total control. This self-identification as oppressed people explains the remarkable decision by Flemish nationalists to draw parallels between themselves and the Congolese, as is the case in the pamphlet "De Vlamingen aan de Negers van den Congo" (1885; The Flemish to the Negroes in the Congo). The pamphlet argued that the exploitation of the Flemish was comparable to that of the Congolese: both were victims of Belgium's French-speaking bourgeoisie and its powerful ally, the royal family. When Congolese visitors to the World Expo in Brussels in 1958 were asked to sing a song in their local language for King Baudouin (1930–1993), the journalist Louis De Lentdecker responded with a column in the Flemish newspaper *De Standaard* in which he lamented not being African because, if he were, he and other Flemish visitors to the Expo would perhaps also be allowed to address the king in their own language instead of having to use French.

However, this anti-royalist and anti-elitist attitude should not be interpreted as anti-colonial. Flemish writers frequently used racist stereotypes, such as the "civilized white" and the "primitive black", in order to establish a hierarchy vis-à-vis the Congolese. Although they compared themselves to the Congolese, Flemish nationalists did not question the superiority of Western civilization. The parallel rather served as a way to distinguish themselves from the nation's French-speaking bourgeoisie. By portraying themselves as "the blacks of Belgium," Flemish nationalists primarily dissociated themselves from the patriotic rhetoric of Belgium's francophone elite.

Missionary Zeal

Paradoxically, the ambiguous sentiment in Flanders about Belgium's colonial ambitions was accompanied by a strong admiration for the numerous Flemish missionary workers in the Congo. The vast majority of the Catholic missionaries operating in the colony were Flemish. Although Dutch was never used for missionary activities, the anti-French sentiment among many of the missionaries was reflected in their eagerness to convince the Congolese to take pride in their native languages, which stimulated identification on the basis of African language groups. Significantly, indigenous languages play an important role in the famous study *La philosophie bantoue* (1945; Bantu Philosophy) by the Flemish missionary Placied Tempels.

The interest of Flemish priests in African languages, culture, and history could also be part of a missionary strategy. A well-known case is that of Jean Cuvelier, the bishop of Matadi, who studied the history of the ancient Kingdom of Kongo under the Catholic African King Afonso I (1456–1542). Cuvelier's discovery that Central Africa had a (largely forgotten) Catholic history dating back to the fifteenth century was of great importance to Belgium's missionary ambitions in the region, where there was fierce competition between Catholics and Protestants for the souls of the Congolese. In his eagerness to show that Catholicism had ancient roots in the Congo, Cuvelier displayed a tendency to make the kingdom look more Catholic than it had actually been and largely ignored the fact that what had developed in Kongo was a uniquely African variant of Catholicism, characterized by a syncretic mixture of Catholic Portuguese and indigenous Kongolese elements.

Of all Europeans living in the colony, missionaries were the ones who had the most contact with the Congolese and often an intimate knowledge of indigenous culture. Hence, it is not surprising that Africans are the main characters in a number of literary works written by missionaries. A well-known example is Adolf Verreet's paternalistic novel *Het zwarte leven van Mabumba* (1935; The Black Life of Mabumba).

In their writings, missionaries often struggled to find a balance between their fascination with indigenous cultures and their awareness that, as a result of their missionary activities, the alleged cultural authenticity would necessarily disappear. The psychological portrayal of a black man who in order to become a Christian has to relinquish his beliefs and traditions forms the core of Alfons Walschap's short story "Longwangu de smid" (1933; Longwangu the Black Smith). Ultimately, Longwangu is converted to Christianity, but the preceding conflict makes his conversion all the more nuanced and thus all the more credible.

The tendency in Flemish literature to glorify the simple, "pure" life in a rural environment as opposed to the "decadent" lifestyle of the urban (and predominantly francophone) elite can also be found in the missionary and colonial ethos. Much Flemish literature on the Congo is characterized by a certain ambiguity. Writers glorify the European civilizing and Christianizing mission in the colonies, yet at the same time admire the alleged authenticity and purity of indigenous life. A reflection of this ambiguous attitude is the tendency to depict "civilized blacks" (*évolués*) who rejected their indigenous culture and adopted a Western lifestyle as morally decadent. Some examples can be found in the anthology *Kongo ya lobi* (1961; The Congo of Yesterday). This jubilee issue of the colonial periodical *Band* offers a sampling of Flemish literature on the Congo. In a number of short stories, the authors present African culture as primitive and seem convinced that there can only be improvement in the lives of the Congolese if they adopt Western standards of civilization. However, whenever a Congolese, attracted by the glitter of urban life and seduced by the European way of living, leaves his village to go to the city or even travels to Belgium, he is always disadvantaged. The message is unequivocally clear: Africans can only find true happiness, love, and tranquility in their "traditional" village communities. Thus, the continued superiority of the colonizers is guaranteed.

Few people in the deeply Catholic Flemish society doubted the noble intentions of the missionaries. The profound entanglement between the Catholic Church and the colonial administration remained overlooked in Flanders, where people massively collected aluminum foil and put coins in money boxes in the shape of an African boy to support the building of (Catholic) churches, schools, and hospitals. *Blanke boeien* (1934; White Shackles), a novel by Jan Schoup, exposes these opposing interests. The novel is a fierce indictment of the mining companies, the local authorities, and the colonial government, who are all portrayed as undermining the great work of the missionaries. In *Blanke boeien*, Father Versteeg is engaged in an unequal battle which he can only lose. His valiant efforts are to no avail and his work remains fruitless. Eventually, he loses his life.

While works such as *Blanke boeien* express a critical perspective on Belgium's colonial policy, they do not question the foundations on which the colonial constructs are built. The objective of colonization is not rejected — only the way in which the colonial administration is trying to achieve it. Although they have serious misgivings about the methods used, the writers still identify with the primary aim of colonization. Another example of this attitude is *Oproer in Kongo* (Revolt in the Congo), written by the well-known author Gerard Walschap after his return from a visit to the Congo in 1951 where his brother Alfons, whom we discuss later in this book, worked as a missionary. The novel provides a cross section of colonial society, with a rich plantation owner, a missionary, and an *évolué* as the main characters. Each is given the opportunity of pleading his case. Walschap describes how the black revolt irrevocably changes the relationships between the characters. He denounces the exploitation of the Congo. The plantation owner then has to return to Belgium and is replaced by his son, who believes in a new approach. Johannes, the *évolué*, is promoted to head of the workforce. With this rearrangement of the relationship between the colonizers and the colonized, and the recognition of the humanity of the Congolese, everybody is satisfied. Walschap's unequivocal signal to the reader is that a different attitude is urgently required. Yet his call for colonization with a human face does not fundamentally alter the balance of power in the colony.

Anti-Colonial Voices

It would nevertheless be a mistake to assume that no anti-colonial voices could be heard in Flemish society. For instance, in his satirical *Verslagen over den Gemeenteraad van Nevele* (1885; Minutes of the Municipal Council Meetings of Nevele) and *De zwarte kost* (1898; Eating Black), Cyriel Buysse deliberately debunks the colonial ethos. In *De zwarte kost*, the local bourgeoisie of Akspoele is the butt of Buysse's criticism because of its narrow-mindedness, arrogance, and ignorance. In this novella, Western civilization is not worth its name; the Europeans are the real barbarians, who can offer the Congo nothing but misery and hardship. Buysse also denounces the colonial propaganda, which played on the exotic appeal of the Congo, the prospect of a life of adventure, and the ideal of bringing Western civilization to an allegedly backward continent. In *De zwarte kost*, the motives of the colonizers are unmasked: they are driven by self-glorification or base instincts and not at all by humanitarian concerns. At a time when the colonization effort was still in its infancy, Buysse already publicly declared its bankruptcy.

In 1898, the year that Buysse published *De zwarte kost*, the Dutch author Henri van Booven left for the Congo in the service of a Dutch trading company. His novel *Tropenwee* (1904; Suffering in the Tropics) is the only work included in this anthology that was not written by a Flemish but by a Dutch author. It vividly describes the horrors awaiting Europeans in Central Africa. *Tropenwee* is the account of the trip to the Congo undertaken by a certain Jules. The closer he gets to the tropics and the more the heat increases, the more his unease and discomfort grow. As soon as he has arrived in the Congo, his superior sends him into the interior. On the boat on the Congo River, he is weakened by malaria and dysentery to such an extent that he has to return to Europe. The middle section of the novel consists of the hallucinatory nightmares of the main character. The last part describes the harrowing return trip. Only when Jules gets closer to the north do his energy and strength return. *Tropenwee* is the description of a descent into hell; the writer paints an evocative and haunting picture of Jules' excruciating spells of fever during this voyage on the Congo River. For Jules, Africa is a threat, as the heat, the insects, and the storms make his life unbearable. In no way is the presence of Europeans in Africa justified. Not a single word about the civilizing mission is mentioned. Only commercial interests seem to motivate the presence of the Europeans in Africa.

Tropenwee is a fierce indictment of the fact that the suffering, the diseases, the greed, the inhumanity, and the deaths of innocent victims resulting from the exploitation of the tropics are swept under the carpet. As in Buysse's *De zwarte kost*, the Africans figure only in the margins of the novel. They do not form a counterweight to the depravity of the Europeans. Van Booven does not idealize Africa or the Africans. He only focuses on the presence of Europeans in Africa. From his perspective, Europeans cannot adjust to life in Africa; Europe has nothing to offer to Africa but avarice and greed, while Africa is nothing but disease and death to Europe. This sobering assessment leaves no room for colonial triumphalism and renders any alibi for colonial imperialism null and void. Despite this fierce anti-colonialist message, the novel became a bestseller in Flanders and the Netherlands.

René Poortmans picked up this anti-colonialist thread in the 1930s. His novel *Moeder ik sterf* (1937; Mother I am Dying) is an outright attack on the cruel exploitation of the Congolese by the mining companies. The tropics affect the Europeans in such a way that they lose all sense of morality. The words of the title – "Mother I am Dying" – are pronounced by a black man and express the fate of the Congolese. The novel ends with the following bleak assessment: "One drifts from Europe to a post; and from the suffocating post in the heat back to the lifeless, petrified Europe. Lost on both sides."[4]

In 1959, Piet van Aken published his novel *De nikkers* (The Negroes). Meersman, the administrator of a district and the main character of the

---

4   Poortmans, R. *Moeder ik sterf* (Antwerp: Belgische Uitgeversmaatschappij, s.d. [1937]), 224.

novel, relates the events surrounding a strike by Congolese workers. However, the focus is not so much on the strike itself. Indeed, the Europeans are more concerned about protecting their privileges than about the strike and the frustrations of the black workforce, whom they disparagingly refer to as *nikkers*. This shift in focus from the central incident to what is taking place on the periphery of the strike is an illustration of colonial policy itself. Van Aken characterizes the colonial situation as one of misuse of power, in which the ruler suppresses the colonized without mercy. Even though the novel ends in a confirmation of the status quo, there is also a subtle suggestion that the balance of power will not last forever. In *De nikkers*, the legitimacy of the colonization project is undermined, and the emphasis is on the nature of man itself.

3. The Postcolonial Period

The Trauma of Dipenda

In the late 1950s, the process of decolonization took on unstoppable momentum. In 1959, riots broke out across the colony. The Belgian political establishment capitulated quickly and granted the Congo its independence. On June 30, 1960, the colonial period came to an abrupt end. At that time, many Belgians still lived in the Congo. Shortly after the independence celebrations, heavy rioting erupted, which resulted in a large number of Belgian casualties and triggered a mass exodus. In the following decades, a series of violent upheavals, armed conflicts, and bouts of civil war led to the departure of almost all Belgians from the Congo. Only a handful of missionaries remained.

Upon arrival in Belgium, many ex-colonials recorded their experiences of the violent upheavals following independence. In most of these works, the authors look back with nostalgia, puzzlement, and embitterment on a period which was closed off forever. *De rode aarde die aan onze harten kleeft* (1962; The Red Earth Which Clings to Our Hearts) by Daisy Ver Boven, *Zonen van Cham* (1964; The Sons of Ham) by A. Claeys, *Ik blanke kaffer* (1970; I White Negroe) by Paul Brondeel, and *Djiki-Djiki* (1972) by Jan van den Weghe make up just a small selection of titles inspired by the brutal beginning of Congolese independence. Most of these authors were eyewitnesses who were caught up in the violence themselves. In their novels, the Congolese are frequently cast in a negative light while the Europeans are seen as the innocent and defenseless victims of raw racial hatred.

A Clash of Cultures

The violence that marked the period immediately after independence squarely confronted the Flemish with the dismal failure of the colonization and civilization project. This led to a great deal of soul searching. Several authors examined the universality of Western values and reflected on the problem of acculturation. In their work, they often focused on the problematic relationship between white and black interracial couples. Novels such as Raf van de Linde's *De Moeloeba Catteeuw* (1965; The Muluba Catteeuw), Jan van den Weghe's *Offerhonden van stro* (1965; Sacrificial Dogs Made from Straw), Albert van Hoeck's *Over de grens* (1970; Across the Border), and Daisy Ver Boven's *Mayana* (1974) dealt with this subject matter. For a number of writers, the impossibility of establishing a permanent loving relationship illustrated the unbridgeable cultural gap between black and white, Africa and Europe.

The clash between African and Western culture is most acutely expressed in the person of the *évolué*. In Jef Geeraerts' *Ik ben maar een neger* (1962; I'm Just a Negro) and *Het verhaal van Matsombo* (1966; The Story of Matsombo), the *évolué* Grégoire-Désiré Matsombo is a medical assistant, the highest degree to which a Congolese could aspire. Geeraerts portrays him as an opportunist without a moral compass. Not surprisingly, both stories end negatively. The bankruptcy of both Western civilization and African culture is expressed in no uncertain terms by the figure of Matsombo. In Geeraerts' eyes, Western society is depraved, while Africa conjures up a paradisiacal prehistoric world and Africans are supposed to assume the role of noble savages. As argued by the literary critic Ton Anbeek, "[Geeraerts] ridicules the black *évolué* not because he is black but because he wants to be white. Because in order to do so he has to abandon the blissful primary state of thoughtlessness. Every *évolué* is, in Geeraerts' eyes, one too many."[5]

The Legacy of the Missionaries

The belief in the integrity of Flemish missionary work in the Congo has not necessarily waned as a result of steady secularization in Flanders since the 1960s. Even among secularized Flemish there were and remain some voices

---

5   Anbeek, T. "Het donkere hart. Walschap, Geeraerts en de Kongo", *Ons Erfdeel* nr. 38.01 (1995): 85.

carrying forward a vision of the Congo that reduced Flemish involvement in colonialism to charity and blaming all negative aspects of Belgium's colonial history on the country's French-speaking bourgeoisie and royal family.

An interesting consequence of this selective remembering of Belgium's colonial history is the lack of inhibition in the Flemish media and among Flemish politicians when it comes to denouncing acts of corruption and oppression involving the post-independence Congolese political leaders. This led to the remarkable decision by Congolese expats in Belgium to wave Flemish flags during demonstrations in 2012 as a way to express their discontent with the political regime in the Congo as well as their support for the harsh tone used in the Flemish media when addressing corruption in the administration of the Congolese president Joseph Kabila. It reflects a paradoxical – and to outsiders completely obscure – form of postcolonial solidarity between descendants of the colonizers and the formerly colonized.

The fact that the majority of Belgian missionaries who remained in the Congo after the country's independence originated from Flanders contributed to the legacy of missionary work becoming an important topic in postcolonial Flemish literature. For instance, this is the case in the work of the missionaries Jac. Bergeyck and Guido Tireliren. Bergeyck, who worked in the Congo as a missionary from 1947 to 1959, was intrigued by African indigenous culture. His anthropological interest and research were directly transferred to his literary work. The most striking characteristic in Bergeyck's prose is his empathy for the Congolese. The author situates the latter within their cultural "traditions" and pays little attention to political or social developments.

The legacy of Catholic missionary work is also a prominent topic in Flemish travel writing, most notably in the work of Lieve Joris. Joris has close ties with the Congo: her great-uncle was a missionary there. In her travelogue *Terug naar Kongo* (1987; Back to the Congo), she describes a visit to the Congo in the footsteps of her great-uncle and explores contemporary Congolese reality. She describes and tries to understand the Congolese and their society:

> In that sense I am of the opinion that the postcolonial generation has a duty, the duty to show how different things are now. I went looking for Congolese intellectuals. Because I wanted to know how they think about their country

and how they look upon their youth. I wanted to find out what we as whites had meant there. ... I think we are the first generation that can look at it in a detached way.[6]

Joris' Congo book is a kaleidoscope that deals with a broad variety of topics, from the nostalgia of the missionaries and the daunting problems of a country where little is still in working order to the widespread corruption. She also discusses the clash between long-held traditions and the new norms and values. Furthermore, Joris stresses the vitality and hospitality of the Congolese. She knows that she is looking at the Congo through Western eyes, but precisely this awareness and her sustained attempts to dig beneath the surface allow her to examine the complexities of the Congo. Her trip is an expedition that explores not only the present but also the past. It traces the history of Belgium's relationship with the Congo, which leads to a multifaceted picture of a complex interaction in which the African is empathetically present. *Terug naar Kongo* is a fascinating travel book, which sheds new light on a familiar subject matter. In *Dans van de luipaard* (2001; Dance of the Leopard), *Het uur van de rebellen* (2006; The Rebels' Hour), *De hoogvlaktes* (2008; The Plateaus), and *Mijn Afrikaanse telefooncel* (2010; My African Telephone Booth), Joris gave voice to her lasting fascination with the Congo. With her books, she inspired David Van Reybrouck, who in *Congo: Een geschiedenis* (2010; The Congo: A History) returned to the country where his father had once worked as an engineer.

In the novel *Afrika retour* (1993; Africa Retour) by Markus Leroy, cynicism prevails. The main character is the head of the Belgian Department for Development Cooperation in an African country, which can easily be recognized as the Congo. Due to corruption in the Congolese government and political interference by Belgian diplomats, no effective development aid can be provided. Only a cynical attitude allows the main character to survive in such an immoral environment. *Afrika retour* is a scathing novel in which there is no room for postcolonial guilt and remorse, let alone hope. It is the final nail in the coffin, not only of colonialism but also of postcolonial "development" ideology.

---

6   De Moor, P. "Terug naar Kongo van Heeroom: Interview met Lieve Joris," *HN Magazine* (April 25, 1987).

4. Conclusion

Flemish literature on the Congo has received little scholarly attention in Flanders and abroad. Even literary scholars have neglected most of these works. In fact, existing overviews of Dutch literature pay scant attention to colonial and postcolonial literature about the Congo. This attitude reflects a problematic tendency among literary scholars to determine the importance of literature on the basis of (subjective) aesthetic norms. While it might be true that, from a purely aesthetic point of view, much of Flemish literature on the Congo is relatively poor, its focus on Belgium's colonial past makes these prose works singularly important.

As we have argued, Flemish literature on the Congo cannot be properly understood without taking the social and cultural specificities of Flanders into consideration. Yet while these authors were naturally marked by a Flemish worldview and by Flemish moral concepts, much of the literature they produced was born out of tensions provoked by the culture shock they experienced upon arrival in the Congo. While some tried to deny these tensions and remained stubbornly attached to the colonial and missionary ethos, others made the former the main topic of their literary work.

In light of the fact that all the authors writing colonial literature were white and that the Belgian Congo was a highly segregated colony, the absence of the colonial "Other" in much of Flemish literature on the Congo is not surprising. It would therefore be wrong to assume that by reading this literature one will come to a better understanding of the Congolese. These works, as a rule, tell us more about the authors themselves – their identity, mentality, and culture – than about the Congolese.

There can be no doubt however that the Catholic missionary activities in the Congo represent an important and long-lasting legacy. The way Flemish society perceived the Congo was strongly shaped by missionaries. Of all colonials, they were the ones who stood closest to the Congolese people and who had an intimate knowledge of local culture and language. It is therefore no surprise that some of the most intriguing Flemish literature on the Congo can be found in the context of the Catholic mission. The constant tensions between the attachment to a colonial system of exploitation on the one hand and Christian charity on the other, or between the Christianizing goal and the fascination with the cultural wealth of what was presented as "indigenous traditions," are at the heart of much Flemish literature on the Congo, even if written by secular authors.

These were the tensions that ultimately forced Flemish authors in the Congo to debate the essential question: Why are we here? In the postcolonial era, this question was either put in the hypothetical form (What if...?) or the past tense (What remained?). An additional element that became centrally important in reflecting on the Congo was the topic of guilt. It confronted writers with the question of whether present and future Flemish generations should feel guilty for the colonial exploitation of the Congo, in particular the horrors that occurred during the reign of Leopold II. Writing about the Congo in the postcolonial era implied a reflection on how Flemish society should deal with Belgium's colonial past.

Up to the present day, the Congo continues to be an important topic in Flemish media. The success of Van Reybrouck's bestselling historical study indicates that even younger generations of Flemings with no direct connection to the former colony still show an interest in a country and an era they only know from stories told by their parents and grandparents. It can therefore be assumed that, in the coming decades, the Congo will remain an important topic in Flemish literature and society. With this anthology, part of these reflections on the Congo in Flemish literature can now be shared with an international audience.

PART 2
SELECTED EXTRACTS OF FLEMISH PROSE

Aldemar-Camille van der Cruyssen

A Peaceful Crusade

Aldemar-Camille van der Cruyssen (Nevele 1836 – Antwerp 1926) was a writer and primary school teacher. He began his teaching career in Nevele, where one of his pupils was the author Cyriel Buysse. In 1861 he moved to Courtrai, where he became acquainted with Hendrik Conscience, arguably the most influential Flemish author of the nineteenth century. Together with Conscience and Hugo Verriest, Van der Cruyssen was on the committee of the Literary Society of Courtrai. He is the author of morality tales and contemporary sketches, a play, an essay about his native language, and a description of *Gheel, de kolonie der krankzinnigen* (1923; Gheel, A Shelter for the Mentally Ill).

His most eloquent and passionate book is undoubtedly *Afrika, naar de beste bronnen* (Africa, on the Basis of the Best Sources). It was published in 1877 and fits perfectly into Leopold II's strategy of promoting to the Belgian population the acquisition of a colonial possession. Eight years later, the king became the sovereign of the Congo Free State. Van der Cruyssen's most forceful argument for colonization, namely the moral obligation on the part of the European nations to bring civilization, Christianity, and commercial development to Central Africa, was used time and again by the civil and religious authorities during the colonial era.

Van der Cruyssen's description of Africa is profoundly Eurocentric. *Afrika, naar de beste bronnen* advocates for the submission of Africa and the African to Western civilization and, thus, considers the colonial conquest of Africa inevitable. After an overview of the available information on the different parts of Africa, the author deals — in the last chapter called "The Trade in People" — in highly emotional terms with the slave trade in the Sudan, Upper Egypt, and Central Africa. He claims that the situation in Central Africa is by far the most desperate and requires urgent intervention. The rather businesslike account in the previous chapters is suddenly replaced by a barrage of words. An accumulation of exclamation marks, ellipses, and rhetorical questions reinforces Van der Cruyssen's plea for European intervention. After a heart-rending description of the inhuman fate of the slaves, the chapter ends with an appeal to Europe for solidarity with Africa.

> **Extract originally published as:**
> Van der Cruyssen, A.-C. *Afrika, naar de beste bronnen* (Courtrai: Ch. Vandesteene, 1877), 142–44.

Africa, on the Basis of the Best Sources

Let us now raise the question: Isn't it high time to put an end to all these injustices? Shouldn't a way be found to put an end to all those horrible things? Shouldn't every clear-thinking human being lend a hand to help his brothers in these unfortunate regions, to support them and free them from the claws of unscrupulous rascals and lowly villains? Yes, well, this must end! This disgrace should no longer be tolerated by civilized humanity.

Let's unite behind the noble ideal of our King! Let's do whatever we can to make this project flourish! Let's hope that it will bear good fruit, will open Africa to us and introduce our deplorable brethren to general civilization.

This will be so, and this will be achieved by neither force nor violence. We shall operate peacefully and not as conquerors among these people.

In the heart of the country, wherever there is a chance of success, we will establish posts, which will appear as beacons of light among these unfortunate people and we will make our beneficial presence felt quickly.

Their presence alone will keep the slave traders under control, and when the African people know that they can live free and in peace, they will slowly begin to make progress, and the seeds of Christianity and of European civilization will not fall on barren land.

Roads will be constructed, and, in this way, products will be easily transported to us; who knows, perhaps in some years from now, this rich land will be known as the most extraordinary storeroom of Europe!

For this, powerful support is needed; and such support will be provided for our project. Significant sums have been collected, which already generate an income of more than 100,000 francs per year.

And this is only the beginning; because could anything be more beautiful, or could anything more honorable be done, than contributing to the liberation, the ennoblement, of one's fellow man? Yes, it will be a general crusade, no longer with the sword in hand, but with words of peace and conviction, with feelings of love in the heart, and with self-sacrifice in the soul!

Cyriel Buysse

White Depravity

Cyriel Buysse (Nevele 1859 – Afsnee 1932) was a major Flemish novelist and playwright in the naturalistic and realistic mode. Buysse's first published literary work is the novella *Het Erfdeel van Onkel Baptiste* (The Inheritance of Uncle Baptiste), which appeared in 1885. Earlier in the same year, however, he had distributed the fictitious *Verslagen over den Gemeenteraad van Nevele* (Minutes of the Municipal Council Meetings of Nevele) on stenciled sheets in his village. The work consists of five short discussions between Nevele's council members, dated between January 1885 and June 1886. They poke fun at the councilors by exposing the absurdity of their argumentation. At the meetings of April 9, 1885, and June 15, 1886, the Congo is the most important item on the agenda. These minutes are considered the first Flemish literary texts on the Congo Free State.

In the novella *De zwarte kost* (1898; Eating Black), Buysse returns to the topic of the colonization of the Congo. This time, he directs his mockery at the inhabitants of Akspoele, a small fictitious Flemish village, from the self-important dignitaries to the uncouth whitesmith. The main character is the stuttering Fortuné Massijn, the clerk of the village notary. He invites two black princes, who are being educated in Flanders, to visit Akspoele. The visit goes disastrously wrong, after which Massijn decides to leave for the Congo. After his departure, his letters keep the villagers informed about his experiences in the colonial possession of Leopold II. The extract in this anthology is taken from Massijn's report of his arrival in the Congo. He quickly comes face to face with the fact that the Europeans behave in an all but civilized manner. They drink to excess and are obsessed with sex, to which the novella's title alludes with the expression "Eating Black." Massijn too succumbs to the temptation to enter into a relationship with an African woman, but in contrast to his fellow Europeans, he truly loves his Congolese girlfriend. He dies eleven months after his arrival in the Congo Free State.

In *De zwarte kost*, Buysse criticizes the colonial propaganda, which plays on the exotic attraction of the Congo, the lure of an adventurous life, and the ideal of bringing Western civilization to Africa. Buysse unequivocally questions the reasons for colonization and the motives of the Belgian colonizers.

Extract originally published as:
Buysse, C. *De zwarte kost* (1889), in: *Verzameld werk 4* (Brussels: Manteau, 1974), 441–45.

Translated with permission from the Cyriel Buysse Genootschap.

— Eating Black

Another fourteen days passed. Then, one morning, the mail carrier from Bavel delivered a second package of strange letters to Akspoele. These had stamps on the cover with the image of King Leopold and had been postmarked in Boma. And, from then on, they came regularly, every fourteen days or three weeks, and also became gradually more interesting.

While Fortuné was still in Boma, waiting until the caravan with which he would travel into the interior was finished with its final preparations, he had received an answer to his first letter from Mr. De Vreught, his former teacher. And now that the journey had started, he often made use of the evening quietness in his tent to write to his friends in Belgium, and to make up for the way his stories in his first letters were all too dry by writing more picturesque and anecdotal ones.

In the beginning, these letters had been full of glow and enthusiasm; oh, the scenery was beautiful and wonderful in Africa; it was an unending Eden, in which people lived like gods. Then that passion began to gradually weaken, betraying a compulsion, a forced enthusiasm to keep up the optimism; and an increasing disappointment could clearly be read between the lines. There was one morning, some three months after Massijn's departure, when Mr. De Vreught received a letter from him expressing pessimism and disillusionment that could no longer be controlled.

"Dear teacher," he wrote to his retired teacher, "I simply have to pour out my heart to you. To my home and to Eulalie I consistently write cheery letters in order not to disappoint them; but I have to tell you, in all honesty, that everything in this country has certainly not been as rosy as they think in Belgium, and that many ugly and sad things happen here which should not happen. And this is how it is: the Europeans, who supposedly came here to civilize the savages, generally bear the greatest responsibility for this misery.

Some days ago, our caravan, consisting of two hundred porters, a dozen native soldiers and five white travelers, had stopped at nightfall close to a village. As the place seemed suitable, the commander decided to camp there. Dinner was served, as usual, in the large tent; and, after much was eaten and drunk (since, teacher, you have no idea of the amount drunk by the Europeans here), each of us went to his own tent to sleep.

All had gone quiet in the camp, and in deep sleep I lay resting from my exhaustion, when a crazy roar of screaming and gunshots suddenly woke me up. With a yell I jumped up, grabbed my rifle, and ran half-dressed outside, followed by my boy who screamed as if he were being murdered.

Lights whirled around wildly through the camp, half-naked men ran between the tents, an intermittent musket volley sounded at a distance of fifty paces and – accompanied by shouts and oaths – was enough to curdle your blood.

It was the natives of the nearby village storming the camp. That lasted around a half-hour in a roar and confusion that had no equal. Then everything went quiet. You heard nothing in the dark night except for the awful moans of the injured and dying.

Still entirely aghast, and fearing that there were dead among our white travelers, I fled to the large tent, where we had dined the previous evening. Immediately I saw my fear was unfounded. My four white fellow travelers stood unharmed around a table with two burning candles. They laughed exuberantly when I came in, and, while a boy put two bottles of champagne and glasses on the table, I noticed, to my surprise, by the flickering gleam of the candles, four half-naked women in a corner of the tent: four young Negroes who, trembling and crying out in fear, stood closely together. Baffled, I kept staring at this scene from the entrance of the tent. Then I asked what had happened, why the natives had attacked the camp.

'Oh, see here's why… Because we wanted to have some fun,' the head of the caravan answered, with a finger gesturing to the Negro women. His face, fixed on me, had a mocking expression.

'Say then, were you the only one who stayed single tonight?' he joked.

I'll let you imagine, dear teacher, how indignant I was. I bowed without saying a word and left the tent. But only the following morning I learned the whole truth: the gentlemen had ordered the four women from the village to be kidnapped, and the natives had stormed the camp in vengeance. And that is what one in Belgium calls civilizing the savages! You know what they've learned fairly well from our culture, teacher: swearing and drinking gin. Whenever they have to make an effort, to carry something heavy or to row fast, the 'fucks' and 'shits' roll out of their mouths. They swear like devils, dear teacher; and, concerning the gin, as soon as they can get hold of it they just drink it up until they drop. In my opinion, teacher, these people were much happier before they knew our civilization. But divine justice punishes the kinds of abominations the Europeans commit here. All those who surrender themselves to alcohol and 'eating black' will before long become victims of their own misdeeds. The dreadful climate of Africa punishes their excesses with a death warrant, as is certainly appropriate.

Let me now tell you, dear teacher, about another case.

It happened the day before yesterday, during a stop of our caravan at a trading station near the shore of the river. I'd prefer to not mention names of places or people; a letter can get so easily lost in these savage lands, and here, just like in Belgium – and maybe even more so than in Belgium – there is much jealousy and slander. Anyway, dear teacher, to cut a long story short, here's what happened:

When we arrived there we saw a small steamboat lying next to the dock of the trading station and about to leave for Boma. There were various white passengers on board, including the head of the trading station, who, after finishing his term of three years, was returning to Europe. He is, by the way, a married man in Belgium and a father of four children. We had boarded the steamboat to see off our departing compatriots, and we had just returned to the caravan, which was resting on the shore. Suddenly, while the steamboat was leaving the dock, we heard a fearful scream from the top of the rock inclining over the river. Terrified, we raised our eyes, and saw on the point of the rock, just on the edge of the abyss, a woman, a young Negress, who, begging and crying with gestures of despair, stretched out her arms to the departing ship, while holding a small child. And suddenly, at the very moment two Negro men rushed over hoping to grab her, she made one last scream and jumped more than one hundred meters into the river with her child…

At that place, teacher, the water of the Congo tumbles into wild-foaming whirlpools over a bed of sharp rocks. Even the strongest swimmer would have difficulty saving himself there. None of our men, despite their courage, dared jump in the water. Four of them quickly got in a canoe and paddled with all their strength fifty meters downstream, where the unfortunate woman, carried away by the wild river, surfaced momentarily, still holding her child in her arms. But all rescue attempts were futile. After about an hour of searching, they had to give up. So now, teacher, you probably want to know who the woman was and why she jumped in the river… She was the concubine of the head of the trading station, the man who is married in Belgium, father to a family; and she took her own life and killed her child, his child, because he refused to take her along with him on his journey back to Belgium.

P.S. Many greetings from your best friends, the young princes Albert Badoe and Boudewijn Soera. You can only imagine how happy they were when they saw their fatherland again. Yet it is unfortunate that they almost immediately got so frightfully wild again. It is as if the veneer of civilization, which they brought back from Belgium, had suddenly been taken away. They have already fought three times with other boys of their age, and before their departure from Antwerp it had been necessary to take away the revolvers they had received as a present, because they used them to shoot at the porters. They also don't want to speak a single word of Flemish or French, taught to them with so much effort, any longer. They continuously speak and scream in their wild language instead. I am very afraid, dear teacher, that our civilization has made no more impact on them than rain on a duck's back."

Pieter Danco

A Mini-Europe in the Tropics

Pieter Danco (Antwerp 1871 – United States 1952) is known for his sentimental poetry and prose, such as *Jubelzang der kinderliefde* (1892; Ode to Parental Love), *De familie van den werkman* (1893; The Family of the Workman), and *De roode haan* (1898; The Red Rooster). Danco lived in Boma, the capital of the Congo Free State, from 1893 to 1896 and was the secretary of Governor-General Wahis. He is the first Flemish author with personal Congo experience to use the colony of Leopold II as the setting for a literary work. The novel *Ook een ideaal* (Also an Ideal) was published in 1896 and awarded a prize in a competition held by the Davidsfonds, a Flemish Catholic cultural organization. After his return to Belgium, Danco voiced his strong support for the African possession of Leopold II in a speech given to the Geographical Society of Antwerp in 1897. In 1900, he was appointed European director of the Belgian-Congolese company Urselia. In that capacity, he revisited the Congo in 1902 to inspect its plantations.

Ook een ideaal is a hyperromantic love story, set against the background of the construction of a railway line through the Lower Congo from 1890 to 1898, an endeavor which claimed a large number of lives. Officially, 1,800 black laborers and 132 European supervisors died, although the real death toll is probably much higher. In the novel, Helene Hoogenbosch and Hugo von Litze fall in love with one another. She is a Catholic girl living with her uncle, Mr. Smitz, in Matadi. The latter is the manager of a Portuguese trading company. Hugo von Litze is a German engineer working for a company building the railway line between Matadi and Leopoldville. This railway link is vital for the economic development of the colony's interior, as rapids on the Lower Congo prevent navigation on it. In contrast to Helene, Hugo von Litze is not religious. He is very ambitious: his role model is Ferdinand de Lesseps, the builder of the Suez and Panama canals. After a number of dramatic incidents, such as a revolt by Senegalese railway workers and the collapse of the bridge Hugo is building, Helene succeeds in converting Hugo to her Catholic ideal. Together they return to Europe, where a great future awaits Hugo.

In this story, the Congo functions as an exotic location. The Europeans have turned it into a mini-Europe, with the same class distinctions and conventions of etiquette as on the old continent. The Congolese only appear in the margins of the story. *Ook een ideaal* makes it abundantly clear that, from the beginning of the colonization, European interests are paramount. The first encounter between Helene and Hugo and the polite conversation between Smitz and Delois, a manager of the railway company, takes place at the beginning of the novel.

Extract originally published as:
Danco, P. *Ook een ideaal* (Ghent: A. Siffer, 1896), 15–20.
Translated with permission from Standaard Uitgeverij.

Also an Ideal

The clock above the counter in Smitz' dining room struck six.

Night began to fall.

Helene switched on the lamp, closed the shutters, which were covered with tulle, in front of the open windows, and then cast one more glance at the table to make sure that Bomala, the Negro girl, had laid it out properly.

She seemed satisfied after her inspection, because she patted Bomala's black curly hair and smiled warmly at her. The Negro girl looked up happily at her mistress, and when she smiled, she let two rows of pearly white teeth shine between her lips.

Helene deeply loved Bomala, especially because she felt strongly drawn to those who had less luck in life.

Bomala was a Negro girl from the area of the Inkissi River. Her father had been one of the best *capitas*, or chiefs of the porters, in the service of the State; yet, after frequently walking the distance from his village to Matadi with a heavy load on his head, he had felt broken. He was one of the first natives to realize that the civilization which the sons from the chilly North had brought to the children of the warm South was a blessing: that they had come out of love for their fellow men and not out of greed, to impart the light which radiated from the North, and to make them enjoy the advantages of material and spiritual development and progress.

When he felt broken and realized that his days were numbered, he brought his daughter, his dear Bomala, to the Sisters at Kinkanda to make a decent woman out of her, just like the white women were. Then he laid down his weary head and, as a Christian with true neophyte belief, departed to his Savior.

For around four months now, Bomala had been with Helene, who had done her best to continue the honorable task of the Sisters, to wear away the primitive native husk of the child and to complete her education.

Her work had not been in vain: after all, the young Negro girl reciprocated the interest her mistress had taken in her with heartfelt devotion and almost slavish attachment. The gratitude that Bomala showed her was the only reward Helene desired; she was one of those noble spirits who devoted themselves completely to a labor of love, not thinking about profit or gain, but only about love toward a suffering human being. Helene's heart had become as pure as gold in the crucible of suffering. Since then, she felt the need to spread the healing power of her compassion to all those around her.

That is why she had adopted the poor Negro child and had given her all the love she held so deeply in her heart. The realization that she at least made someone happy gave her satisfaction and peace.

"Bomala," she said, "I am happy with you, everything is in order, you deserve a lot of praise, child."

Then she heard steps on the veranda; the door opened.

"Ha!" Smitz said, while he stepped in, "our young mother is again opening her heart to her adopted child. Helene, here are our guests, as I am bringing another one along…"

"Yes, Miss Smitz," Delois interrupted, "I have permitted myself to bring the son of one of my old friends here. Let me introduce him to you: Hugo von Litze, chief engineer for the railroad company; he has been in Matadi for just one month." "Hugo," he continued, turning to the young man, "this is Miss Smitz, the niece of my best friend here, a gem of a girl, and the best housekeeper that I know."

Delois was on very familiar footing with Smitz. He shook Helene's hand with a friendly squeeze. Helene likewise extended to Hugo her hand, which he shook.

She didn't seem as sad as she had been in the afternoon; there even seemed to be a light blush on her cheeks which took away, or at least hid, all the dejection which had been there lately.

"Pleased to make your acquaintance, Miss Smitz," said Hugo; "it is a delight we don't often get to enjoy here in Africa – we miss it so often, we might even be underestimating the value of finding ourselves in the company of women."

Helene was somewhat embarrassed by these flattering words and didn't know how to answer. Smitz immediately saw this, and interrupted:

"Now, is dinner ready? ... Yes? ... So, then we can take our seats at the table. Although, now that they're in Dutch territory, the gentlemen will probably have a drink first?"

The bottle of liquor was already waiting, and, a couple of minutes later, the four of them were sitting at the table.

Hugo von Litze, whom Delois had introduced to Smitz, was German by birth, but had been brought up by an uncle in Holland after he had lost his mother and father at the age of four. After finishing his engineering studies in Leiden in brilliant fashion, he journeyed to other countries to learn new things and quench his insatiable thirst at all the fonts of learning. He had visited Belgium, Germany, England, and America in turn. Everywhere he had learned new things, and had mastered more and more of the secrets of science. So he had become an experienced man of great knowledge, a master of his profession. Nowadays he held the position of chief engineer at the railway company in Matadi.

There he felt at home.

With heart and soul, he devoted himself to the great work that was planned and completed here, where he could quench his thirst for knowledge and bring to fruition the plans he had devised earlier while studying and visiting various engineering masterpieces. With courage he took up the task of wrestling with nature in the wild, of clearing a way along a wall of rocks and to build his railway on it, to cross the vast gaps, to build bridges over deep abysses, rivers, and streams, and to drain the swamps – in short, to take up and execute great works with great courage.

This was his goal, his only desire.

Dinner was very pleasant. After the meal, tea was served. Smitz and Delois had started to discuss business.

"See," said Smitz, while he offered Delois a cigar and lit one up himself, "the advantage for our company is this: we can force the porters, which our recruiters send from Luvituku to Matadi, to accept new terms, which would decrease their pay if they bring their loads only to Nkenghe and no further, or go there to pick them up. This would make using the railway profitable for us, since the distance between Nkenghe and Luvituku is only a few days of walking." "Still," he continued, shaking his head, while he stirred the sugar in the tea, "they won't! The natives prefer to come to Matadi, and they consider the relief of having only to walk to and from Nkenghe too small, and not in proportion to the decrease in pay the company would impose on them."

Delois found some truth in this, yet couldn't keep himself from arguing for the company and to glorify all the golden benefits of using the railways.

Pieter De Mey

A Giant Step for Civilization

Pieter De Mey (Wetteren 1862 – Antwerp 1918) was a journalist who wrote a number of travelogues: *Van Antwerpen naar Stanley-Pool. Reisindrukken* (1899; From Antwerp to Stanley Pool. Travel Impressions), *Naar 't land van de middernachtzon: reisindrukken uit Zweden en Noorwegen* (1906; To the Country of the Midnight Sun: Travel Impressions from Sweden and Norway), and *Het land der sluimerende millioenen* (1904; The Country of the Dozing Millions). He made a short trip to the Congo in 1898 for the inauguration of the above-mentioned railway. Only two years after Pieter Danco had returned to Belgium in 1896, the railway line between Matadi and Leopoldville was completed. Its solemn inauguration took place on July 6, 1898, in Leopoldville. The official opening was a grand affair. The guests included representatives of the Congo Free State, the Belgian Government, the army, the religious authorities, commercial interests, the shipping trade, the press, and diplomats from a number of European countries. All travelled by ship, the *Albertville*, from Antwerp to Matadi and from there by rail to Leopoldville. Among them was Pieter De Mey.

The participation of journalists in the trip fits perfectly into the public relations activities of the Congo Free State. De Mey is indeed full of praise for Belgium's undertaking in the Congo. He repeatedly asserts that the Belgians are engaging in an effort that puts the neighboring colonial powers, France and Portugal, to shame. De Mey praises the colonial pioneers for their dedication, self-sacrifice, and entrepreneurial spirit. He is convinced that the Belgians who died in the Congo will be revered as saints by future generations of Congolese.

Van Antwerpen naar Stanley-Pool is written from a lofty Eurocentric vantage point. De Mey's travelogue sketches a positive picture of the colonization and, thus, contributes to the myth of the colonial enterprise as a benevolent undertaking. De Mey describes in detail the inaugural festivities, which culminate in a solemn banquet that features a black orchestra playing Western music. After the banquet, which was characterized by the inevitable self-congratulatory speeches, a native allegorical procession takes place, depicting the speed at which the Congo is embracing European civilization.

> **Extract originally published as:**
> De Mey, P. *Van Antwerpen naar Stanley-Pool* (Turnhout: Joseph Splichal, 1899), 230–35.

From Antwerp to Stanley Pool. Travel Impressions

And now the solemn gravity gave way to a more festive atmosphere, and one hundred sixty white people lined up around the table to conclude the inauguration of the railway with a European feast.

The space on the veranda was taken up by a band of young Negroes from the mission in Boma, who played excellently under the direction of one of the Brothers. In this way Africa and Europe were already working together as brothers.

A feast always requires a toast. We thus followed the ancient custom, and Mr. Fuchs drank to the King, after which the young Negroes played the Belgian national anthem.

The emotion and enthusiasm that burst out when they played the *Brabançonne* are impossible to describe; it can only be understood by those who have actually experienced something similar so far away from home.

General Daelman, the representative of His Majesty, expressed his gratitude for these generous words and promised to convey these feelings of patriotism to the King.

"Today," he continued, "will be one of the most remarkable in the history of Middle Africa. It has sealed, in fact, the occupation of the mysterious interior by civilization, which the King said 20 years ago was the only place on the globe that civilization hadn't permeated."

After some observations about the large, just finished task, he wished, in the name of the King, all prosperity to the rail line and welcomed the dawn of a new era for Africa.

Then Colonel Thys stood up and, with his well-known rhetorical talent, delivered a beautiful extemporaneous speech.

He said: "The day after tomorrow, the trains, which brought you to Stanley Pool, will carry you back to Matadi. Before the end of the next day, we will all be able to see the endless horizon of the sea again.

After these few days spent on African soil, what will leave the strongest impression on us? Which memory will remain etched the deepest in our hearts and souls?

Will it be the memory of the Belgian general, who, as a sign of great devotion, laid on the Banana Peninsula a cross on the grave of his only son, who gave his life for his country?

Will it be the sight of the stately Congo River, winding along the green plains near its mouth, so wide and large that it almost gives the impression of infinity?

Will it be the emotion felt during the landing at Boma and the inspection by the representatives of the king of the small African army of the State? Or maybe the pious modesty at the *Te Deum*, sung in the presence of the representatives of almost all the powers of Europe, on the 13th anniversary of the foundation of the State, followed by a flawless parade of the black troops, accompanied by the sound of trumpets?

Will it be the spectacle that same evening in Matadi, brilliantly lit, the city only recently risen from the soil, or rather from the rocks, and from now on designated as one of the greatest trading centers in the world? Or the striking spectacle of the crowds of black workers, who with cheery songs celebrated the completion of the great endeavor, and thus glorified a cultural achievement, accomplished through hard work and determination?

Will it be the memory of what we experienced in Tumba, of the Africa of yesterday, primitively rough and poor, that came out to greet with respect the Africa of tomorrow?

Will it be the great endeavors of the railway company, the memory of the difficulties overcome and the progress yet to come?

Will it be the surprise that you must have experienced when in Leopoldville you discovered a nascent city created at the initiative of your compatriots?

Will it be the visit to Brazzaville, the memory of the banquet tonight, where one saw in mysterious Africa the purple of the prelate next to the white shoulders of the ladies and the embroidered outfits of the diplomats and representatives of the world's most powerful nations?

Undoubtedly, all of you will be led by your character and your feelings in choosing this emotion. As far as I am concerned, my choice is made; the most powerful emotion I experienced during this journey was the conviction of the still greater and increasingly powerful European occupation. This had already impressed me before – today it is the most powerful emotion. There is no doubt anymore: Africa has been won for civilization! You have seen it, just as I have, after your stay in Boma, not only in the work that has already been completed, but also in the concern for the future revealed in the schooling given to the children. Your conviction was reinforced in Matadi by the remarkable development of all types of businesses and institutions in this city. This was confirmed during our railway journey, which thoroughly proved itself in the immense endeavor of leading this country from barbarism to civilization – with a gigantic opening up to the world at each end!

My conviction was strengthened even more upon seeing the developments in Pool, and, as though in a dream, I foresaw the time, within some years, when its shores would be covered with wharves, like the large cities of America, born from the cooperation of business and industry.

All of this has convinced me that a gigantic task is being completed here and that it won't be long before one will greet the new world of Africa. The ideas of the King, and their execution, will have a dominant impact on the final decades of this century.

For such great things to be achieved, a strong administration is needed. It will be one of the greatest merits of the King to select with the greatest care the men needed for this task.

Mr. Governor, you stand at the same level as your predecessors (*long ovation*). These ovations prove that my audience agrees with me. These words of praise are not the common official ones, but expressions of my conviction. It is with these feelings that I raise my glass in your honor.

Ladies and gentlemen, to the health of the Governor General of the Congo State!"

A long ovation greeted these words, and it was with profound emotion that Mr. Fuchs thanked the brilliant orator and gave a toast to him and to his administration for obtaining this victory for modern enterprise.

Count d'Ursel concluded by thanking the representatives of the friendly nations for the applause with which they had toasted to the King and had drunk in the name of our country to their prosperity and to the further development of the world in terms of work and progress.

Knight Mauriq von Sarnfeld delivered a toast to the members of the press with flattering words, after which Mr. Tardieu responded with a lively toast to the role of women in bringing civilization to Africa.

Hear in the distance a trumpet resounds, and, on the street in front of the veranda, lots of people were moving around. It was a torchlight procession of Negroes who were also celebrating the inauguration. Suddenly, all my fellow diners left the table to watch this remarkable spectacle.

There, the beautifully lit and allegorical procession came to a halt. In front were two Negroes carrying a banner attached to two sticks with the year 1888 printed in black numbers. After them a Negro chief followed in national costume, seated on a litter carried by slaves. He depicted the situation in 1888.

A second group, similarly preceded by a banner but with the year 1898, showed a Negro in modern European clothing, which represented the progress made in the last ten years by civilization in Africa.

Both groups were surrounded by countless Negroes with burning torches.

One could find this performance overdone, and, with regards to the Negroes, this was somewhat true, but, if applied to the Bas-Congo region, it was quite accurate.

The spectacle was very remarkable and the Negroes had enjoyed themselves a lot.

Now, on the shores of the Congo, beautiful fireworks started, which at that place could certainly be called an extraordinary performance.

Dead tired after such a busy day, and before the end of the fireworks, I wandered along the sandy slopes of Leopoldville to the station, because we needed to return to Kinshasa to spend the night and then continue our journey to Tumba the following morning.

At a certain moment, I left the beaten path. I found myself entirely alone in the high grassy fields, while the last fireworks split the darkness and cast a shadow over the tropical landscape. It was like an image of the task of the whites in Africa: here, the wilderness, the dark desolation; and somewhat further down on the shore of the river the rising, shining light. The distance was short, but the difference was enormous.

Constant De Deken

A Missionary with a Cause

Constant De Deken (Wilrijk 1852 – Boma 1896) was a missionary of the Order of Scheut. Before moving to the Congo, he had been a missionary in China, an experience that led him to write *Dwars door Azië* (1899; Straight through Asia), about his adventurous trip through Mongolia, Tibet, and China. His next challenge was a journey to the Congo, undertaken rather unwillingly as he had not yet fully recuperated from the exertions of his Asian adventure. De Deken accompanied his superior, Jérome van Aertselaer, along with three missionaries of Scheut and five Sisters of Love. The Order of Scheut had been active in the Congo since 1888. In *Twee jaren in Congoland* (1900; Two Years in Congoland), De Deken recounts his trip, which lasted from June 1892 to October 1894.

The travel account was first published in instalments in the French and Dutch edition of *Missiën in China en Congo* (Missions in China and the Congo), the periodical of the missionaries of Scheut. In November 1895, De Deken returned to the Congo with the goal of establishing a mission at Riba-Riba on the Lualaba in Maniema and improving the transport of goods to the different posts of the missionaries of Scheut. He fell victim to a tropical disease and died in Boma in March 1896. In 1904, a statue in honor of De Deken was erected in his place of birth, Wilrijk, near Antwerp. Sculptor Jean Hérain represented De Deken as a colossal missionary towering over a half-naked Congolese man, who raises his hands in a gesture of supplication toward him.

During his trips through the Congo, De Deken made use of steamships, the only means of transport allowing relatively easy access to the interior. He always found himself surrounded by Europeans and expressed the utmost admiration for the military personnel and representatives of the Congo Free State. He considered them courageous pioneers who were bringing civilization to the Congolese and examples of heroic self-sacrifice, a phrase that echoes throughout the travelogue.

From De Deken's perspective, colonization brings nothing but good. He ignores or minimizes the destructive impact of the European presence on the Congolese communities. For example, when some of the black crew members of the steamer he is travelling on are struck by smallpox, they are left behind on the shore of the Sankuru, a tributary of the Congo River. Their presence there leads to the spreading of the disease across the whole region, resulting in countless victims. De Deken, however, is not in the least taken aback by this tragic turn of events.

Extract originally published as:
De Deken, C. *Twee jaren in Congoland* (1902), in: *Twee Jaar in Congo* (Antwerp: De Vlijt, 1952), 87–90.

Two Years in Congoland

As a reward for my efforts, and to help me recover from the difficulties endured, they prepared a tasty cocktail in my honor, an incomparable drink to give the exhausted explorer new strength immediately. To make it, you beat the whites of a dozen eggs to foam; you scramble the yolks; you add a good quantity of sugar, with gin, cognac or champagne. You can refine the taste with what the English call "mixed spices," or simply with nut spices. On Olympus, the wine of the gods was drunk, but scholars lost the recipe for it; I am convinced that the English found it again and that the wine of the gods was none other than this cocktail.

That evening, while we were playing cards by the light of two candles, a nightly ritual, we were tormented by thousands of insects – moths, night flies of all sorts, winged ants, mosquitoes, beetles, day flies – all of which were attracted to the flame and burnt up in it until the candles petered out.

The following morning we were required to take strong action against our loggers, who had done almost nothing the entire night. Commander Gillain divided them into three groups: the ordinary loggers, the soldiers who had come from the camp in Kinshasa in support of the superintendent, and the other black travelers. Each of these groups had to procure a certain quantity of wood; otherwise they were not allowed to eat the entire day, and no hippo meat whatsoever if any were shot during the journey.

After we resumed our journey, we soon reached a large marketplace, held on the shore. We bought many nice things: weapons, carved figurines, fabrics. The earlobes of the women had holes large enough to fit a five franc coin into. In these, they hung flowers or little shells, which in many places in Africa are used as small change.

Here I must recount the saddest incident of our whole journey. You'll remember that, among the one hundred children who came from New Antwerp to complete their military and scholarly education in Boma, I had selected two servants in Leopoldville who would accompany us, along with Mangunga and Nganza. The little black one, chosen by me to serve the Right Reverend, was already baptized, and called Fataki. The boy must have come too close to the hospital in Leopoldville, where several patients had smallpox when we departed. When he arrived there, the poor young black boy got an intense headache and felt great fatigue in all his limbs. Two days later, his whole body was covered with marks of the terrible disease. In order to avoid infecting our entire staff, we were required to isolate the boy and to lay him in the dinghy which was dragged behind our ship. We regularly gave him food and drink, and we kept some of the best scraps from our table for him. Two days after the bumps appeared, he was hideous; from head to toe his whole body was just a horrible purulent scab.

We thought he wouldn't escape death. But how tough is a Negro? He spent day and night lying in an open boat, under heavy rainfall or incessantly splashed with the water churned by our boat, having no way to shelter from the burning rays of the sun. Such circumstances would make the toughest child in Europe collapse ten times over. Fataki, however, bore all those sufferings with extraordinary courage; after ten days the crusts fell off, his appetite returned and the poor sufferer, who was annoyed that he couldn't play with his friends anymore, received permission to return aboard. Disastrous carelessness! Not even three days later, a dozen adult Negroes were in turn affected by the disease. Among the sick were stokers and mechanics, the under-captain's servant, and the young wife of the helmsman; in short, the infection would keep spreading if we remained, God knows for how long, anchored there. The dreary prospect was that the entire crew could die. We then opted for the lesser of two evils and left all those suffering from smallpox behind. We provided them with a sufficient quantity of exchangeable goods to sustain themselves for at least three months by trading with those living on the shore. On the way back from Lusambo, the vessel would pick them up again.

This sad departure was equally painful for the Negroes as for the Europeans who remained on board. Those left behind were their fellow workers, compatriots with whom they hoped to return to their region of origin soon. Among them was also the boy from the tribe of the Bangalas who cooked for everyone. Those poor black people cried so much when we put sixteen of their companions on the shore, some of whom appeared to be close to death! Still, we had to leave, our hearts filled with fear and sadness.

Alas! We were not at the end of our sufferings. Four days later, we had to leave another eleven men behind, and among them were various people whom we needed to keep the ship going. An inevitable consequence of that situation was that we often had very little wood to burn in our boiler. And the captain, who now had only an unskilled stoker and mechanic to count on, only dared to sail on half steam power and on certain days used the engine for no more than two hours.

In addition, the remaining staff was so disheartened that they could hardly do any work. Thankfully, Commander Gillain is a man of many skills, and I don't know what would have become of us without his clever and brave intervention. First and foremost, he replaced the captain, a Dutchman named Boerhave. This man, also infected with smallpox, had become blind and crazy from the disease. Judge De Saegher tasked himself with his care, but the unfortunate Dutchman suddenly appeared – despite his blindness – in his no-collar shirt on deck and started shouting all sorts of orders with a loud voice. They brought him back to his cabin and carefully locked the door. Ten minutes later, he came back, probably through the window, and acted in the same way.

On another day, the first mechanic, M. Kiles, from Liege, lay dying from fever and bloody urine. Thinking he was near death, he received the last rites. Judge De Saegher went and sat at his side and started injecting him with Cinchona bark. This saved his life.

Are we now at the end of our misfortunes? Not yet: the captain of the "Stanley" was also feverish and saw no other option than to hand control of the boat over to Messrs. Gillain and Fivé. Because of all of this it took us thirty-six instead of twenty days to reach Lusambo.

Later we heard that when the "Stanley" returned to Leopoldville, only sixteen of the twenty-seven Negroes we had put ashore had been found alive. The survivors returned with the ship to their homes. And after our stay in Luluaburg, when we came back along the same route, we learned that there was even more to report in the way of misfortunes.

The inhabitants of that area, allured by the cheap goods which we had left behind with our patients, had been in contact with them, and brought the infection to their own villages. A year later, smallpox still reigned in the area of the Sankuru; ten thousand Negroes had succumbed, and entire villages were abandoned and burned by their inhabitants, who then moved to the shores of Lake Leopold. And when I passed by with the nuns I had to bring from Leopoldville to Luluaburg on the same steamboat, our ship was soon recognized and attacked with arrows and spears, as they believed it had brought the pestilence to the area. We had to take flight quickly, but, before we returned to Leopoldville, the captain devised a ruse, which worked perfectly. His boat always had had a gray color; he had it painted entirely black. With that new misleading cover, the Negroes let the "Stanley" approach their shores in full freedom to buy firewood and goods.

Let us forget about these nasty memories and admire the beautiful vegetation along the shores of the Kassai. One can see wild coconut trees there, whose pliable branches were laden with woolly pods, and snake plants from which rubber flowed and whose golden yellow fruits were competed for by white people, Negroes, parrots, and apes alike. Other trees, covered with blood red berries which made their branches bend, contrasted brightly with the somber green of the woods. And high, very high above all those giants of the forest that shade the impenetrable chaos of thorny shrubs with their wide crown, there rises, straight as a column and covered with a silver bark, a beautiful tree whose trunk, naked until the top, culminates in an awesome sunshade of long, narrow leaves.

Henri van Booven

No Place for Europeans

Henri van Booven (Haarlem 1877 – The Hague 1964) was a journalist, an author, and an avid sportsman who introduced cricket and rugby to the Netherlands. In 1933 he wrote the first biography of the famous Dutch author Louis Couperus, whom he had met at the home of Cyriel Buysse: *Leven en werken van Louis Couperus* (The Life and Work of Louis Couperus). He wrote a number of novels, which either received a lukewarm reception or remained unpublished. He did achieve remarkable success with one novel, *Tropenwee* (Suffering in the Tropics), which was published in 1904 and could be regarded as the Dutch counterpart of Joseph Conrad's *Heart of Darkness* (1899). Both novels have an autobiographical basis and describe a harrowing journey on the Congo River.

In the fall of 1898, the twenty-one year old Van Booven stayed in the Congo for four months. He was employed by the Nieuwe Afrikaansche Handels-Vennootschap (New African Trading Company) and sent to a trading post in the interior. On the steamer headed toward its destination, he got malaria and dysentery, which forced him to return to the coast. Against all odds, he survived the ordeal and was able to return to the Netherlands. The diary he kept provided Van Booven with the raw material for his novel. *Tropenwee* became a bestseller, with no less than eighteen editions before disappearing completely from the literary radar.

In *Tropenwee*, Van Booven testifies to the horrors awaiting the Europeans in the Congo. The main character is Jules. On Congolese soil he is called "the white one," which suggests his unsuitability for life in the tropics. Jules has high expectations of his stay in the Congo but, soon after his arrival, the country turns into a huge threat to his well-being. Africa completely saps his strength. The tropical forest, the heat, the insects, the storms, and diseases make his life unbearable. The Congo has got nothing to offer to him except illness and death. In the extract selected for this anthology, Jules travels the Congo River in a dilapidated boat. At night, he stays in a village along the shore, sleeplessly fighting mosquitoes off from his bed.

In this novel, Belgian colonization gets short shrift. It is presented as a purely commercial undertaking, a free-for-all with no victors. No mention is made of the "white man's burden" or the moral duty of bringing Western civilization to the African continent. Rather, Van Booven demonstrates that the truth about the numerous European victims in the tropics was deliberately concealed in Europe itself. For the fourth edition, which appeared in 1919, two chapters were added to the novel: at the beginning "Op Gran Canaria" (On the Island Gran Canaria) and, at the end, "Thuiskomst" (Arrival). In "Thuiskomst," the Congo Free State is explicitly and severely criticized. With the addition of these chapters, Van Booven wanted, somewhat belatedly, to align himself with the critics of Leopold II.

Extract originally published as:
Van Booven, H. *Tropenwee* (1904), in: *Amsterdam: Maatschappij voor goede en goedkoope lectuur* (s.a.), 16–21.

Suffering in the Tropics

One after another, the memories kept coming back to him in no particular order. There was the day of his arrival in Rotterdam, a sad fall day with dry weather but cloudy skies. He saw many square rough cobblestones, next to each other in the ground; horses that carried slow, heavy, long rattling wagons; and working people, speaking poorly and wearing caps and clothes that were dirty brown in color. Those people spat on the ground and stood by the bridges, sometimes with an arm resting on a handrail, one leg jauntily crossed over the other. They chewed tobacco and spat brown juice on the dry stones, which were dirty and glistened with spit on the spot where they were standing…

It was also the day of the exam; four hours of doing calculations, questions on accounting, and translations in French, English, and German. Not very difficult, and everything was done long before the time allotted for the test…

The gentlemen directors sat there, one a dark, handsome fellow, the other with a blank face. Both faces were hard. These were surely people who had no feelings, knew no compassion. They looked cold and astonishingly indifferent, people who loved numbers, accountants, smart heads among the traders.

The blond one had a large, fat head, which surely must have been full of calculations, and he looked as if he had never known anything besides buying and selling … Ha! Ha! The scoundrel! No, really, never anything besides buying and selling… But nothing of a feverish, buzzing tropical night, nothing of insects in his food and of mosquito bites, of ants and scorpions, of fever and scabies, of eczema, and eye and ear inflammations…

In the large, musty offices of the business partnership, where pale clerks were bent over high stand-up desks, he waited for the old man, the small gentleman, with glasses in front of his green, mean, sneaky eyes. He was the one that would lead him out with the three others to Antwerp. The three others sat staring out dully in front, as if they seldom or never spoke a word, never a serious, well thought-out word. The one with the beard did have something to say. He liked to make jokes, and said that he "was about to return," and that he had been "there" six years already. He spoke to the man with the beard. He asked some things about the country, how far he had traveled. He tried to understand how the work had been distributed and asked about the countryside, about the rivers and trees and the heat and the Southern stars.

To the first questions the man gave no clear answers; he answered as if it annoyed him to have to speak with people so inexperienced about boring daily matters. He already had enough of this and he kept doing it only out of desperate need. But it seemed as if that man had never seen forests or landscapes. He didn't answer those questions, and, when he was asked once again about the Southern stars, he looked dazedly in front of him and started talking about the "lovely girls" – "If you wanted to have a nice girl, then you should take one from the coast. On the coast you find such lovely things. So different and so nice. Yeah, on the coast you can get virgins, thirteen, fourteen years old; in the interior of the country, you don't get any virgins. They are nice and young, for sure! And wholesome and healthy! But … there are no virgins…"

In the train, it was stuffy and smoky. He sat across from the small, old gentleman with the glasses, who had "already" led "so many" away. The old man looked around, cunning and cool, when he had given an answer. It occurred to him that you actually weren't allowed to talk with that old man, the man looked so protective and attentive. He truly looked like a jailer would: watchful, surly, and he gave his answers with a certain reserve, as if he had wanted to say, "You are talking to me, and I'll answer you, but I don't have to. I am your jailer. I don't have to do anything except to make sure that you stay in the compartment. You received a five hundred guilder deposit from the partnership, and you have to give it back to the partnership. You might certainly get it in your head to get out at a local train station, and go and be merry with that money. No, dear friends, I'm here to fulfill my obligation; I will make sure that you stay seated. You may ask as much as you want, just as long as you don't escape…"

Suddenly he saw the heads of the directors again. The heads grew longer and bigger, monstrous in size. The blond looked him straight in the eyes: "You will stay three months on the coast to get acclimatized, then you're going 'further up', if asked by the chief inspector. Understood?" The blond head came close to him and said again sharply: "Understood?" The head was so large, and the mouth so wide open that he feared the director would want to bite him, bite him on his face, and he stretched his arms out to push him off…

Then he felt the tulle of the clammy, greasy mosquito net and he knew he was awake, that he had come back to reality again.

He thought of that, the acclimatization. Instead of three months on the coast, he had been travelling now for weeks, starting immediately after his arrival, journeying from the coast to the interior. Months were lost over there with traveling to and from the coast and the interior, and to and from the trading post and the sea. It was all deceit, lying, and cheating. Could anything have been done? Stand up, complain to the chief inspector? That would lead to nothing. That could hardly improve your chances of even a small promotion. Just hard work and doing your job, being a duty animal, a duty villain, and participating in cheating for the benefit of the partnership and yourself. In this way, everything beautiful disappeared. Nature itself became barren, annoying, even more than annoying. And the black people, they were the black cattle whom you had to be strict with, hard, and cruel; you had to keep them under your thumb, be sure that they wouldn't rob you. With good words? Oh no! With beastly cruelty and with a lot of whipping. Yes, certainly, you also had to become the torturer in the end. You had to beat your fellow man to the point of drawing blood with dried hippo skin, with those hard, long, dirty yellow sticks with which you give beatings, which made entire muscle groups lame … the company shares stood far above par, and above par they would stay. You had sold yourself, you duty animal, duty villain! Duty torturer! And all the profits went to the company! …

He heard the dog very clearly now. He was still fully awake. The dog panted, sighed almost like a human, his collar clattering. He began rubbing himself with his paws.

"Quiet, Cora! Quiet! Do they bite you as well, poor fellow?" The dog sighed, moaned a little, whined softly and fell with his head against the partition, making a pounding noise.

Next to him behind the thin wall he heard Fourneau, who was also still awake and was scratching himself.

Now he felt that itch again. Itching everywhere. He was disgusted with himself; if only he could take a bath tomorrow, not just a little wash with gross river water. But swimming in the river just wasn't possible: the crocodiles were lying in wait in case you went swimming. You were as good as dead, swimming in the river…

Outside the mosquito netting, he heard the mosquitoes buzzing around. They flew around the tulle in swarms; they couldn't get in. Ha! Ha! Nice! Nice! They couldn't get in; at least that gave him satisfaction.

But the whining finally started to be unbearable.

The mosquitoes made various types of noises depending on their size. There were those with a high pitch, as if coming from a small distance. These were high painful screams. That died out, but suddenly a new nagging noise started, somewhat less intense and nasty. Then it quieted a little, and then others came. With each encounter with the tulle, he imagined how they jumped ridiculously, producing a small shriek, high, like the tinging sound of a very, very fine steel spring which vibrates after a quick, careful contact.

A large, fat one came rumbling with weighty whirring. All these mosquitoes had characters of their own, carrying many different combinations of poison and hellish torture. Oh, they were fine, very fine nagging emissaries from a lugubrious place in the area, a tiny, poisonous band from somewhere in an ugly part of the world, where only darkness and dreariness can come to be and continue to exist. And they all did their silly calling in an extremely well chosen and very pernicious way, each had brought a portion of the great disaster, of that rigid misfortune, that had made them and their torturous noises, so insignificant and annoying, grow, expand monstrously into a borderlessness of unspeakable tormenting woe, almost to the despair of madness...

The itch got worse – it was everywhere. On his legs, on his sides, on his chest, on his back. First, he suffered patiently and scratched when the itch came, then he scratched harder, more, more, faster, angrier. It was the ants, the small red ants that also crawled everywhere with a damnable intelligence. Somewhere in his neck he had a raw spot. He scratched there so frequently that in a frenzy he had scratched the scab off last night and now it started itching, inflaming the itch, always more itching, more, more, more. And he scratched and scratched until it became virulently raw with his dirty nails in the wound; it was slippery from foulness. And then the bleeding started, he felt it on his fingers, which became sticky.

And again he lay still a long time, again and again meekly scratching if he itched somewhere, but always harder, a more intense scratch, until the bleeding began, which felt good. But suddenly in a near frenzy, he flew up, looked for the candle and the matches. This couldn't be, the wounds stung, they needed some coolness, some moist freshness, and he yanked the mosquito netting apart. Somewhere in his luggage was a solution of sublimate. He sprinkled some on the wound, the entire bed, including the greasy sheets.

O, damn! That stung, that really hurt ... and once more, he closed the tulle and burned the couple of mosquitoes who had flown in, and he lay waiting until that one sly one began stirring and he helped that one into death … and then, yes, then it was done, the body was tortured and lay powerless and exhausted, barely feeling…

Eyes half open he saw a glowing beetle sneak in between the cracks of the cheap cabin. It slowly turned around, throwing light on the walls, lazily wheeled around, stayed sitting while emitting light, quiet, on the mosquito net…

A little glowing beetle, a little firefly; far away in the North a symbol of luck, a bringer of luck…

The startled mosquitoes buzzed around…

In dull drifting numbness, he could hear the eternal, hot noise of the tropical night for a long time, wide and starry, the profound secret darkness of the night that buzzed, whizzed, whirred…

Then came the stupor, as if he wallowed with large curves down in a pond and he drifted away in a deep dark sleep…

Henri Bossaerts

White Injustice

Henri Bossaerts' (Pulle 1879 – Antwerp 1934) *Herinneringen aan Congo* (Recollections of the Congo) was published in 2007. The book has a long and remarkable publishing history. It has for its basis Bossaerts' diary for the period 1904-1907, when he was a civil servant working at the court of Boma. Although it was originally not his intention to publish the diary, he changed his mind in 1920 due to circumstances he explains in the foreword to the manuscript. By that time, he felt that the Congo could no longer be compared to the country it had been at the turn of the century; rather, civilization had taken root, changing the Congo for the better. Bossaerts wanted to remind the reader of what the Congo had been like in the early days of Belgian colonization. But his publishing plans were thwarted. Only in 2007 was the manuscript finally published.

The delay in publication was not Bossaerts' intention. The more so that *Herinneringen aan Congo* could, from a present-day perspective, only be read as grist to the mill of the critics of Congo Free State and, thus, as a grave indictment of Leopold II. In fact, Bossaerts' defense of the colonial regime turns into a self-accusation, much in the same way as Mark Twain made Leopold II into a cruel tyrant in *King Leopold's Soliloquy* (1905). But while Twain deliberately put incorrect arguments into the king's mouth, Bossaerts was blissfully unaware of the implications of what he was putting down on paper.

The lofty, idealistic convictions of Bossaerts are in sharp contrast to his actions as a representative of the colonial government. His unshakeable belief in the civilizing mission and the wholesome presence of the Belgians in the Congo shows that he took the pipedream of the civilizing colonization for reality. The utopia in which he believed acquires, on the African continent, all the characteristics of a dystopia. As a result, *Herinneringen aan Congo* provides a revealing insight into the unpalatability of colonial reality. The extract we chose for this anthology recounts the interrogation of a number of black villagers who had killed a cruel colonial administrator. By making false promises, the "man of the court" manipulates the villagers into relating what happened, after which they are taken prisoner.

Bossaerts is of the opinion that the Europeans play an emancipating role in the Congo despite the fact that an individual colonial may on occasion overstep his bounds. Precisely because they see themselves as participants in a civilizing crusade, the colonizers are convinced that they hold up the highest moral and ethical standards. However, in reality, they operate in a moral vacuum, as is evident from the reaction of the Congolese to their presence and impositions. *Herinneringen aan Congo* unintentionally reveals the pernicious consequences of an unwavering belief in the superiority of Western civilization.

Extract originally published as:
Bossaerts, H. *Herinneringen aan Congo. Désiré Bossaerts ambtenaar in Boma (1904–1907)* (Antwerp: Manteau, 2007), 102–08.
Translated with permission from Standaard Uitgeverij.

Recollections of the Congo

The interrogation started with Madumba.
   Q. "What's your name?"
   A. "Madumba."
   Q. "Who am I?"
   A. "You are Tala-Tala, the white judge."
   Q. "Did you know white Dombe?"
   A. "Yes, white Tala-Tala."
   Q. "Was white Dombe good for the blacks?"
   A. "Oh, yes, Tala-Tala, very good even."
   Q. "Did you also know white Malu-Malu?"
   A. "Yes."
   Q. "Was white Malu-Malu also good for black people?"
   A. "No, Tala-Tala. He was very bad, bad as a leopard for black people and especially for the women."
   Q. "Do you realize who I am and what I have come here to do?"
   A. "Yes, white man, you are Tala-Tala, the white judge who came from Europe, from far away over the sea, to see us and give us *matabiches*."
   Q. "Do I have a good reputation among the people of your tribe?"

A. "No, not so much."
Q. "Why not?"
A. "Because we fear Tala-Tala."
Q. "But I'm not causing any suffering or pain, am I?"
A. "Yes, you are. You take our men to Europe to put them in chains."
Q. "That's not true, I only take those who kill others and then eat them. Tell me straight away, where are the two white people Dombe and Malu-Malu?"
A. "I don't know that, Tala-Tala."
Q. "How come you do not know that? Madumba, be careful not to lie to me because otherwise I will have to take strong measures against you."
A. "I'm not lying, Tala-Tala."
Q. "Tell me then, what has happened to the two white men?"
A. … (no answer).

I repeated two, three, four times the same question, empathetically each time, and still no confession. Then I called Banka, Mudu, Bikudili, Tatu, Kadanda and Balaka, put them in line next to each other and commanded they look directly in my eyes, and at the same time asked:

Q. "Did you all know the white people Bombe and Malu-Malu?"
A. (all) "Yes, Tala-Tala."
Q. "Where are those white people? Don't lie, because those who lie will be punished. Tell me the whole truth then and everything you know about it."

After I had spoken, they start arguing with each other; meanwhile, I ask my interpreters to listen closely with me. The disputing and brawling doesn't stop, it keeps going. Chief Matumba Balu wants to meddle in their disputes and discussions, but, in a stern voice, I forbid him to say another word. With great reluctance, he obeys my prohibition and, with angry looks, watches his men. After twenty minutes, I ask for silence and put all the women and men in line next to each other again. My interpreters tell me the results of their eavesdropping, and I restart the interrogation. I start with Balaka because, during the interrogation, he seems to be somewhat honest, and I have the impression that he knows a lot. So, I ask him:

Q. "What is your name?"

A. "Balaka is my name."

Q. "I have just learned that you know a lot about the two white men."

A. "Yes, white Tala-Tala, I am no liar. I am Balaka. Those others are my brothers. Malu-Malu made us harvest a lot of rubber, five hundred baskets. Those baskets were very large (he pointed to one basket that could hold some twelve kilos of rubber). We had to fill those baskets ten times per month. We didn't manage that because the rubber got scarce. The white Malu-Malu got upset because of this and hit us with a whip."

Q. "How much did the white man pay you for the rubber?"

A. "He didn't pay us but gave us a lot of whippings, very many whippings."

Q. "Didn't the white man hit you because you didn't want to harvest rubber?"

A. "No, Tala-Tala, we told Malu-Malu that there was barely any rubber left to find, and he got angry. He had already killed so many women and children and chopped off their hands. Once he put four men and women behind each other and killed three people with one shot. This was to test the gun he just got from Europe. Another day Malu-Malu reproached his soldiers because they didn't kill enough men and killed too many women. Afterwards his soldiers started to kill only men and cut off the genitals to prove to the white men that they killed men. As a reward the white man gave rice and pepper to his soldiers and praised them highly for their bravery. Another day, white Malu-Malu had all our homes burned and killed all our children who were within sight to avenge the fact that we had gathered so little rubber. Then he punished both the men and the women, bound their hands together, placed them on a block and, using the butt of his gun, hit so hard that their wrists broke. The black people cried with pain. The white man, seeing and hearing this, then continued to cut off their hands, which fell on the ground."

Q. "What were the names of the black men, your brothers, whose hands were cut off?"

A. "Mokara, Kivungula, N'Gouna, Palaba and many others. The white man killed Mokara, Kivungula, N'Gouna and Palaba with his gun because they cried almost the entire night from pain, because their hands were chopped off. Once Mokara was dead, Malu-Malu took his two wives and spent the night with them. In the morning he tied these women to a tree and killed them with his gun. All my brothers currently present can attest to such things. If white Tala-Tala allowed me, I would say other things, but I am afraid that Tala-Tala will punish me."

Q. "Balaka, I promise you that you will not be punished if you tell me everything you know. No harm will come to you. Tell me what else you know now."

A. "I am still scared of you, Tala-Tala."

Q. "Why are you scared of me?"

A. "Because you will take our chief and his women back with you and put us all in chains. Doing this will bring you no luck."

Q. "If you tell me the whole truth, I will immediately free your chief and his women. Tell right now what you know about the two white men."

A. "Yes, white man, listen to what I know. I'll suffer nothing if I tell you everything?"

Q. "Again I guarantee that no harm will come to you if you tell everything that you know and don't lie to me."

A. "Tala-Tala, I have known the two white men Dombe and Malu-Malu well, because I was white Malu-Malu's boy. White Dombe was a good white man to us all, but Malu-Malu was very bad. Dombe was of a gentle disposition and good hearted, but Malu-Malu was in contrast a very short-tempered character. The two white men sometimes fought with each other, and it was always Malu-Malu who had to be right. He frequently blamed Dombe for not hitting us with the whip. Dombe answered that such a thing wasn't necessary since whipping caused a lot of pain and no one should be hit that way. Once Malu-Malu was really wound up and he kept whipping us until he got tired of it, and then he grabbed his gun and started shooting anyone who dared approach him. Dombe, hearing and seeing what was happening, took the gun from Malu-Malu, and the two white men started fighting. Dombe got the upper hand and Malu-Malu had to go to bed to get some rest because he was so tired. However, in his wrath he had killed eight black people with his gun, five men and three women. Dombe had a grave dug for them and buried their bodies. On another day, Malu-Malu had all the pregnant women in his post come to him, a total of seven. He tied their hands to their feet, so that they couldn't move any more. He then slept with one after the other, while they were tied up like that. The whole night, these women moaned a lot. Then he killed all the women because, he said, there was not even one who could satisfy or fulfill him. As long as I was his boy, I had to experience all this and be helpful to him. Frequently I was on the point of murdering him since I could no longer bear these tortures. I often spoke with my chief about killing the white Malu-Malu, but my chief told me to be careful, since then the white Tala-Tala would come to take us away and put us in chains or hang us. I see now that such a thing is all too true."

Q. "So you helped in the murder of the two white men?"

A. ... (no answer).

Q. "Well, Balaka, I'm awaiting your answer. Don't lie, and tell me the truth."

A. "Tala-Tala, you promised me that no harm would come to me if I speak the truth."

Q. "Yes, Balaka, and I repeat that promise."

A. "Then I will tell you what happened, Tala-Tala. Malu-Malu had acted terribly and punished many black men unjustly. Four of them were even shot dead. He had whipped me so many times that I cried from pain. This just couldn't last anymore, and we decided to kill him. One night, we assaulted him with around three hundred men. During the fighting, he killed two with his gun, but we managed to overpower and capture him. Dombe, the good white man, tried to get in between and take Malu-Malu's side. We tried to kill Malu-Malu by hitting him with our lances, but Dombe also got hurt and died from his wounds. Malu-Malu, however, got into our hands alive."

Q. "What did you do with Malu-Malu then?"

A. "We killed him."

Q. "In what manner?"

A. "We made him suffer the same pain he caused us."

Q. "How did you kill him?"

A. … (no answer).

At this moment, Chief Matumba Balu made a clear sign to Balaka, which he understood to mean that he should say nothing about the way Malu-Malu was killed. Seeing this, I had him sent away immediately and he was not allowed to attend the hearing of his subjects anymore. This didn't suit him at all and he made strenuous objections. I let him know that, in case of any repeated opposition from him, I would chain him. I forcibly removed him and had him guarded by two soldiers. Then I continued my interrogation of Balaka and said:

Q. "Balaka, listen well. I, Tala-Tala, am asking you for the last time how you killed Malu-Malu."

A. "White Tala-Tala, I will tell you everything, but don't be mad at me and don't punish us."

Q. "Balaka, speak, I'm listening."

A. "When we had captured Malu-Malu, he defended himself with all his strength, to the extent that we had to bind his hands and feet so he couldn't move. Then we stood him up and tied him to a tree, with his arms wrapped around the tree. We cut off his fingers and toes, chopped off his ears and ripped out his beard. Then we plucked out his eyes and tore his heart out of his body."

Q. "Was Malu-Malu still alive?"

A. "When we plucked out his eyes he was still alive, since he cried and moaned from the pain. Then when we carved open his chest, he didn't stir anymore and said nothing."

Q. "What did you do with his eyes and heart?"

A. "The eyes and heart we dried out in the sun. Bika, the favorite wife of our chief, received the eyes as a gift, and the heart we gave to our head captain in memory of his bravery. He still carries it on his chest."

Q. "What did you do with the body?"

A. … (no answer).

Q. "Balaka, I impatiently await your answer."

A. (after a little hesitation and turning his eyes from me) "The body we put in a pit."

Q. "Balaka, you're not telling me the truth. You're lying to me. Speak the truth or I will have to put you in chains to appear before the court of Boula-Matari. Tell me at once what you did with the body."

A. "Tala-Tala will not do me any harm?"

Q. "For the last time, no."

A. "Well, Tala-Tala, we ate the corpse of the white Malu-Malu, because we couldn't satisfy our anger. He had done us too much harm and behaved too cruelly towards us."

Q. "How many of you ate his corpse?"

A. "Many."

Q. "Name the names."

A. "Banka, Mudu, Zimba, Makara, Bandu, Mafuta, Moke, Nivungulu, Badi, Zimbizi, Kivunda, Gombada, and Matari."

Q. "And what did you do with the body of the white Dombe?"

A. "We buried it."

Q. "Where did you bury this body?"

A. "If Tala-Tala wants, I can show him the place where we buried him. It's not far from here."

In order to be sure that what he had told me was true, I did the necessary investigations and, indeed, we found decomposing remains in a pit, covered with leaves and grass.

During the interrogation of Balaka, I had to enforce very strict order repeatedly in order to keep the other blacks quiet. Especially when he confessed that the corpse had been eaten, a strong, threatening movement of dissatisfaction erupted, a general murmur that evolved into screaming. I was able to keep calm and maintain my persistently strict attitude vis-à-vis their chief; this allowed me to instill awe in them and keep them under control. Indeed, my safety hung by a silken thread, and my life floated like a brittle reed straw which threatened to break at any moment. Still I was on my guard. With determination and considerable courage, I interrogated the other natives in succession, and, after I went to a great deal of trouble and exercising much patience, the results of my investigation gave me full confirmation of Balaka's statements. I identified a total of seventy-four people who were guilty of the murder of two white people and twenty-two who were guilty of cannibalism.

Among those responsible were also Chief Matumba Balu and his favorite wife Bika. I placed them all in protective custody and took them away to appear in court.

Leo Bittremieux

Light in the Darkness

Leo Bittremieux (Sijsele 1880 – Boma 1946) was a missionary, scholar, and author. He left for the Congo in 1907, where he remained until his death in Boma in 1946 due to an attack of fever. Bittremieux studied the culture and language of the Bayombe, who live in Lower Congo. He also wrote about his personal experiences as a missionary.

Bittremieux did not doubt the necessity of converting the Congolese to the Catholic faith, being convinced that they could only be saved from damnation if they adopted Catholicism, which would lift their lives to a higher level. He considered superstition and witchcraft the biggest curses affecting the Congolese and their communities. The chiefs and the witchdoctors were Bittremieux's biggest enemies, because they represented the old, primitive ways. Bittremieux rejoiced in the progress the Catholic Church was making in the region, as reflected by the high number of converts.

In his autobiographical books, Bittremieux recounts his experiences as a missionary. *Van een ouden blinden hoofdman, zijn duister begin, zijn veelbewogen midden en zijn gelukkig einde* (1925; About an Old Blind Chief, His Dark Beginning, His Tumultuous Adulthood, and His Happy Ending) is about a chief Bittremieux had personally known and who chose to be baptized on his death bed. *Mayombsche penneschetsen* (1914; Sketches from Mayombe) and *Wit en zwart* (1930; White and Black) show how Bittremieux imagined the daily life of the Congolese people. The books contain a collection of small scenes: how children grow up, the concerns and sorrows of the women, how superstition affects the villagers. With lively colors and sharp outlines, Bittremieux sketches miniature portraits of simple people in the Congo who appear to have the same yearnings as the average Fleming. In spite of his profound knowledge of African culture and society, however, Bittremieux fiercely rejects indigenous beliefs and customs. He equates the Christianization of the Congolese population with their liberation from superstition and abuse. This missionary zeal is ever present in his literary work. In fact, Bittremieux was too much a missionary to be a good writer.

Extract originally published as:
Bittremieux, L. *Mayombsche penneschetsen* (Bruges: Sint Michiel, 1914), 69–73.

Sketches from Mayombe

Do you know the old chief of Tseke-Mbanza? No? Me neither. I've been in his dominion, I slept in his village, but ... no white man has ever seen his face. Our religion teacher is quite friendly with him. He and other black men from near and far tell wondrous things of this old rascal. And, even if it's not entirely true what they say of him, it gives an idea of their slavish fear of a tyrant and their foolish superstition.

That wondrous old man was T'handu-K'oko. He also had two other names, but we'll just call him K'oko.

K'oko is, from what they say, a man of extraordinary dimensions, strongly built and in good shape; but the legs don't do what they could do before; stumbling along is how he walks through the village nowadays. The hairs of his beard and chest are white as snow. The long, frizzy hair – long hair was previously fashionable – of his stalwart head is cut flat by the sickle of time: the lush growth has been made into an arid desert.

No one can really say how old he might be. Certainly he is ... very old. He is, and in the past he certainly was, the greatest chief, the tyrant of the entire region. The black people still respect him as chief, although the State has passed on that honor to one of his subjects and now keeps him on a short leash. All his daughters have died, but he still has sons, and they are no longer young. The current chief of Kivutu is his own child. I saw him: a stout, aged man.

Formerly K'oko bought and caught slaves in faraway villages and sold them God knows where. People say he acquired Tseke Mbanza in exchange for ten men.

He saw the first white men arriving in Boma.

Where he, himself, came from is unknown. He is simply called the "*nkisi*-chief." He must be able to perform magic, must be a sort of spirit! He is feared as much as death is. When he appears at a dispute, everyone gets quiet, from chiefs to common folk. Everyone puts their knives down, takes their headdresses off (if they are wearing them), puts their chairs to the side, sits honorably on the ground, and greets him in the old custom: they rub a little with the right hand behind their head and clap the hands three times repeatedly. The session has now begun. K'oko is the only one with the right to sit on a chair and wear the braided headdress of the chiefs. Whenever there is a discussion, he always out-argues the others. He handles imagery and expressions so well that no one could beat him. Everyone repeats the words that he, in his speech, says first or makes them say... – Who would dare to stand against him? And when the session is over, no one may stand up, not before he does.

Outside Tseke Mbanza he has a type of lordship over Basi Kinanga, which includes some considerable areas of Vaku, K'ele, Sanzulu and over those of Tsinga. There he has the right to appoint chiefs, for the natives at least, and for which he is paid each time with two young slaves, a boy and a girl, without bonuses. Now, however, he doesn't cross the Lukula anymore and usually sends Bula-Matadi from Tseke Mbanza as his representative (the chief appointed by the State).

A miracle man he is. Everything about him is *nkisi* and *taboo*. He eats alone. When he takes his hat off, then his bald head stops the rain! Those who didn't perform the necessary superstitious rituals in honor of a great *nkisi* cannot enter his house. If they would enter anyway, they would die. If he wants to go out on his hammock, he just taps with a piece of wood or a knife on the hammock pole, and the porters make sure that they won't fall during the trip. He has plenty of women, and of all ages. Because he has no intention of dying: "The ones who will have to bury him," he says often, "are yet to be born."

If he saw a white man, then he as well as the white man would die. But then again, he has found a trick against it. Thanks to his *Niondo*, the spirit which protects him – a kind of *nkisi*, which he, like many chiefs, carries in a bag on a string over his shoulder – he could, when the white man comes, sink into the ground, change into a tree, a rock … even into a beautiful youth.

There can be no doubt that K'oko is, indeed, a miracle man! He is a powerful *ndoki*, the black men say, a powerful lord who kills many men, not with a knife or weapon, but through his evil spirits. If he is tired of someone, he sends disease and death to that person's body.

These are unfortunate people who believe all of this deception! May they someday open their eyes to the light of the truth, the light of the Gospel. They groan under the yoke of fear and darkness, under the humiliating yoke of tyranny.

Let us pray and work to hasten that day when they will learn to love and carry the sweet yoke of Christ.

Ernest Tilemans

True Interracial Love

Ernest Tilemans was born in 1884 in Arendonk. In 1911 and 1912, he worked as a civil servant in Matadi and Banana. This experience contributed to his novel *Bendsjé of de liefde der negerin* (1931; Bendsjé or the Love of the Black Woman), about an interracial love affair.

In the Congo, young white colonials often lived with a so-called *ménagère*, a euphemistic term for a black concubine. Such relationships between white men and black women was frowned upon by the civil and religious authorities. If the *ménagère* remained in the background, the relationship was tolerated. If, however, the *ménagère* took on a more prominent position in the life of the young man, the white community took a less charitable view of the partnership, as it was deemed to damage the prestige of the European man and consequently to undermine the civilizing process. In this situation, the colonizer became a man of flesh and blood and was no longer the superior being he should be regarded as by the Congolese. In a colonial context, openly loving relationships between a white man and a black woman and the recognition, with some caveats, of the equality of black and white and of European and African culture were particularly contentious.

In *Bendsjé,* Tilemans' objective was to demonstrate that an interracial love affair leads to nothing but misery. However, he also represents the relationship as genuine, equal, and respectful. Although it is hard to imagine that colonial hierarchies could effectively be transcended in individual relationships, Tilemans, from his perspective as a white male, apparently did not consider that to be impossible.

In the novel's opening, the protagonist, Floris Stockman, is jilted by his fiancée. Distraught, he leaves for the Congo, where he discovers that virtually all Europeans have a *ménagère*. At first, Floris is not keen on following their example. On one of his visits to a village under his supervision, however, he meets Bendjé and is so enchanted by her beauty that he invites her to accompany him on his trips. In this love story, with a murder as a complicating factor, the black woman is presented as sensitive and loyal. She achieves a status that makes the color difference unimportant. For Floris, Bendjsé is the equal of a white woman. This realization also creates an openness toward African culture, which he judges in some respects to be more humane than European culture. By relinquishing the superiority of the colonizer, Tilemans opened up a revolutionary perspective on interracial relationships and on black and white culture, putting into jeopardy the racial premise on which Belgian colonization was based.

Extract originally published as:
Tilemans, E., *Bendsjé of de liefde der negerin* (Brussels: A. Lambrechts, 1931), 79–82.

Bendsjé or the Love of the Black Woman

Soon, Floris discovered that Bendsjé was an extremely lovely human being: always cheerful, happy, and, yes, a bit mischievous in nature. What an enormous difference there was between her and the plump Negroes from other tribes, whom he had met earlier. Her company and her eternal smile were a pleasure. By day, she accompanied him from village to village; by night, after work, she sat next to his lounge chair and rested by his side.

What good fortune had led Floris on that evening to the village where he met her?

Floris had been dazed many times by the splendor of the African country, the majestic magnitude of the Congo River and all the overwhelming new things, which he had been admiring now for fifteen months. Now he found himself in an immeasurable jungle, in the wilderness of the "bush" with its narrow trails, which had remained the same for thousands of years. An indescribable feeling of satisfaction inspired him whenever he traveled through this land in bright sunlight. He felt lucky whenever he trekked through the forests of palm, banana, and coconut trees, or under the wonderful green arch of leaves, supported by thick trunks, tall pillars, connected to each other by proliferating snake plants; lucky to find himself in raw nature, in the African majesty – far from European narrow-mindedness.

In this land, he had met a charming being – a Negro woman – a flower in the wilderness.

Above him the eternal, enormous heavenly torch radiated the whole day – and he, too, felt light and sunny.

He rarely thought anymore about his fatherland, where he had known so much cheating and wickedness. It was now so far away. It was as if he lived in an entirely different world, on another planet.

Bendsjé was a heathen, yes, yet Floris' adventurous nature found no offense in that. He realized quickly that humans, either black or white, differ much less from each other than he first suspected, that all have similar understandings of right and wrong – all creations of the same Creator.

Wishing to learn something more about Bendsjé's family, he asked Pedro to tell him what he knew. Floris had heard that she had been married for some months to the former chief of the village, who had died from an unknown disease. Before this, Floris had already known that, when a Negro dies, his wife or wives belong to the family of the deceased. The surviving wife becomes free again if her family returns the bridal gift which they received earlier. So Floris asked Pedro to explain what Bendsjé's situation was.

Bendsjé's parents, according to Pedro, had died long ago. Her husband's name was Kifuku and he had two brothers, Pamba and Pioka. The older of the two, Pamba, lived in disagreement with both his parents and his younger brother and repeatedly incited the villagers against Kifuku, who enjoyed the support of the State. After some time, the instigator disappeared, and no one knew where he had gone. Some thought he might be a soldier in Angola. After the death of Kifuku, the younger brother, Pioka, a clerk in the service of the State at Banana, was installed as chief. When he was young, he was sent to Belgium, to learn how to become a typesetter. After three years he returned to his country and was employed for a long time as a foreman at the state printing office. He had five wives, one of whom lived with him in Banana, the others in the village; he never claimed Bendsjé as his own. His character differed entirely from Pamba, a wild man.

Floris further learned that Bendsjé must have been around 18 years old.

René Poortmans

Underneath the Leaden Sun

René Poortmans (Heist-op-den-Berg 1903 – Heist-op-den-Berg 1964) studied at the colonial university in Antwerp. In 1927, he travelled to the Congo, where he lived for three years (the regular colonial term). He was stationed as a territorial administrator in Sandoa in the Lulua district in Katanga. After his return to Belgium, he worked for the Socialist Party. Apart from Piet van Aken, he is the only novelist during the colonial era to write explicitly anti-colonialist novels, namely *Moeder ik sterf. Een verhaal uit de Congo* (1937; Mother I am Dying. A Story from the Congo) and *Zon in het zenith* (1939; Sun in the Zenith).

While *Zon in het Zenith* describes the dreadful life of a civil servant underneath the leaden tropical sun, *Moeder ik sterf* is a fierce attack on the exploitation of the Congolese by the mining companies. Both novels have Fred Monsen as their main character. In *Moeder ik sterf*, Monsen leaves for the colony with the ideal of contributing to the civilizing effort but is quickly caught in the colonial web. Although he retains some sympathy for the Congolese and is aware of the hypocritical nature of the colonizing endeavor, he starts behaving as cruelly toward the blacks as the other Europeans. Indeed, the tropics affect Europeans to such an extent that they lose all sense of justice and morality. The colonizers are only capable of taking out their disaffection on the Africans, who are treated as cattle and forced to work for the mining companies as slaves. Over time, the mines require ever more laborers, which results in the rapid depopulation of the villages. None of the Europeans are in the least concerned. On the contrary, government officials willingly provide a helping hand to the mining companies.

In this novel, the Africans are the hapless victims of European indifference and oppression; all they can do is passively submit to their abominable fate. The words of the title are spoken by an African and express his dire situation. Although some Congolese retain their dignity, they behave among themselves as heartlessly and cruelly as the Europeans do toward them.

Moeder ik sterf does not have the evocative power of a literary masterpiece because the main character lacks consistency and credibility. But its highly critical stance on the situation in the Belgian Congo makes it important reading worthy of a wide audience.

Extract originally published as:
Poortmans, R. *Moeder, ik sterf* (The Hague: Servire, 1932), 180–85.

Mother I am Dying

Willey and Frank waited for him at the post.

He looked at Frank, a rough, stupid lout.

"You're a wonderful administrator," he said sarcastically. "All the villages have been abandoned. If you are sent on another inspection, we could move the entire colony to another part of Africa."

Frank shrugged his shoulders. He collected his paycheck, and didn't really care about the rest.

But Willey kept at it.

"You're such a negrophile!" he said and asked about the gifts that had been taken by Africans who had fled.

"You should have taken the tribal chief prisoner. The tribal chief? ... An outlaw chief! ... Then they would have given me my stuff back, for sure."

Monsen looked at him and grinned. He acted confidently. "Go get them yourself, Willey. The chief has neatly laid out all the presents for you. When you come, you will be received with open arms and thousands of Negro women will be awaiting you. But if they eat you, warn them that they should not eat your soul, because then they'll be poisoned."

Their eyes locked into each other; then Willey's eyelids closed half asleep.

"There are still one hundred eighty men left, old sport!" – he said in a yawn.

Monsen had reported the flight of the inhabitants who lived on the border. It was impossible to recruit there and they didn't want a revolt to break out. He had exaggerated these difficulties, hoping to get assigned a lower quota.

The report was a stain on the administration. It disappeared somewhere in the trash. Soon after, a letter from the resident arrived. He wrote that with some goodwill at least five hundred black workers could be gathered.

He wrote: "Work is a blessing for the people. You must clearly see that, with your ideas about civilization. The more inhabitants we pull out of immoral, lazy living, the more their standard of living will rise."

The resident ended the letter reaffirming his trust in Monsen's support.

He didn't mention the border at all.

Desperate, Monsen called Visiri and the tribal chiefs together for an important meeting.

Willey attended the meeting. He was introduced as the agent of the Work Office, and a friend of the white government.

Under a somber silence, the local, native affairs were handled first.

The tribal chiefs spoke, and Monsen listened absentmindedly. He saw Visiri's somber, dark looks fixed on him, and again he also noted the hateful glances fixed on Willey.

Willey sat there, lazy in a chair, grinning, like a ruling god.

At the end of the meeting, there was silence.

Then Monsen stepped forward, and gave a short speech.

"Listen – Visiri, courtiers and chiefs.

The Government has informed us long ago that five hundred men must be handed over to the Work Office this year.

The Work Office clothes and feeds your men well. Where could your men find such clothing and food, here in the savannah?

Many have already left; some willingly, others against their will. The latter are lazy men, who just want to lie sleeping in the sun and let their women work in the cassava fields. All they do is drink *pombe*; they're drunkards. As you know, the Government wants you to work. For all this work, you are being paid in money.

It is a long journey, the journey to the mines. I know that. But we, the white people, also make long journeys to come to you, the Negroes, and give you what you lack.

We come. We don't ask why the government demands five hundred men. It is an order.

When there is a lot of work, there must be a lot of men to work.

You have all been able to see that I behave justly to you all, and I try as much as I can to split the burden equally among all the people.

I went to your rebellious subjects, Visiri, who live at the border, where your authority is sometimes defied. I haven't been able to get one man from them.

Visiri, maybe you have secretly laughed at me in your hut about the refusal of your subjects in the border regions. And you still know that I only wanted to act in a just manner.

Do you always act in this way, Visiri? And you, courtiers and chiefs?

No, I say! Because your rebellious subjects refuse to cooperate, others will have to. I have never led a man away, and I will also never take one along with me. No one has to fear me or flee the village before my arrival. Whoever does that shows that he is disloyal to what the white government asks of him.

Therefore, you chiefs will send your men. I want this to happen.

And I wish for your men to come and report to the white administrators at the Work Office.

Which men, you ask? I will indicate them."

He brought a list forth, on which the names of all group chiefs were written, with the number of men each of them could assemble.

He read this aloud, and concluded:

"Did you all understand me – and will your men come?"

The heads stared out somberly. Monsen became impatient.

"I asked, if you understood me. Do I still need to wait for your answer? Will you send your men?"

They snarled. That meant "yes".

After this speech there was some agitation.

Visiri risked one more attempt, both out of a sense of duty and to justify himself in the eyes of his subjects. He complained.

"Many, many of my children have already left!"

Monsen looked at him, and said softer:

"I know that, Visiri. But what I have decided, I have decided. The number of men I have allotted to the Work Office must come. It's that simple."

Visiri bowed his head, and people left the meeting in a sad mood.

There was no way out. The "young white gentleman" wanted to be obeyed. The Negroes formed groups and fiercely discussed the decision. Poisonous looks shot constantly to the idle, smiling Willey.

Along the road, loud peddling Negro traders squatted with their stuff, with pots and pans and all types of ragged goods, but none of the powerful black gentlemen were paying any attention.

Willey looked at them grinning and turned to Monsen.

"That was Ciceronian, man!" he said mockingly "but most importantly: will they come?"

Monsen followed the black heads with worrisome eyes.

"I will keep them under control" – he said wearily, and left Willey behind.

Willey left, with a smile on his lips.

Jean Gustave Schoup

A Tragic Fate

Jean Gustave Schoup (Antwerp 1893 – Lisse 1944) was conscripted into the Belgian army in 1913. In October 1914, after the breakout of World War I, he deserted during the German army's siege of Antwerp and fled to the Netherlands, where he remained for the rest of his life, earning a reputation as an ardent anti-militarist. His first novel, *In Vlaanderen heb ik gedood* (1932; In Flanders I Have Killed), is an autobiographical account of the first two months of World War I. In the Netherlands, he worked as a journalist and a businessman but he was also a thief, swindler, and counterfeiter. During World War II, he embezzled large sums of money earmarked by a resistance movement to free imprisoned resistance fighters. The resistance killed him in 1944 under circumstances that have never been cleared up.

Schoup wrote four novels, among which is *Blanke boeien* (1934; White Chains). He is also the author of the highly controversial *De geldbronnen van het Nationaal-Socialisme. Drie gesprekken met Hitler* (1933; The Financial Sources of National-Socialism. Three Conversations with Hitler). Schoup claimed to have translated the text but later admitted that he himself was its author.

The main character in *Blanke boeien* is Father Versteeg, a missionary based at a mission post on the Sankuru River, in the country of the Bakuba. The colonizers who have penetrated the area employ the local residents in a diamond concession on the Sankuru. The concession is not successful and is abandoned after some time. Van Dam has to look after the property of the mining company which was left behind. The work on the mining concession has alienated the Bakuba from their traditional activities of agriculture and fishing. After its closure, the Bakuba no longer have any source of income and live in abject poverty. They have been completely abandoned. Father Versteeg feels empathy for the suffering Bakuba and engages his idealism and dedication in the fight against European exploitation and African degeneration. It is not enough to make a difference, however. Eventually, he realizes that his years-long work has born no fruit. Disheartened, he moves to another area where there are no Europeans. There, he loses his life, killed in a raid by Africans from neighboring Uganda. Versteeg is depicted as a martyr, a literary choice that echoes the widespread assumption in Flanders that the missions represented a positive aspect of colonization. The struggle of Father Versteeg against the almighty mining companies and the collaborating civil authorities has a tragic undertone because he is acutely aware of the futility of the fight he is waging. Nevertheless, he soldiers on.

Extract originally published as:
Schoup, J. *Blanke boeien* (Velsen: Schuyt, 1934), 62–66.

White Chains

Van Dam has recovered. Or, at least, this is what he tells himself and what he tells others. But in the evening, when he stands alone on his deck, he can be honest with himself. And then he feels just how weak he still is. He still hasn't been able to drink his regular ration of whiskey, his daily quantity. Also peculiar is his disgust at the first glass. Before, he could feel a strong desire for a drink during the day, and his first glass was a total pleasure. Now, he drinks to fool himself that he can still tolerate alcohol and because of his former habits. In his worst fits, he scolds the priests.

"Those hypocrites with their sparkling water have radically addled my taste... but I will get used to it again..."

It also isn't going well with his eating. In the past, a lot of canned meat in a spicy sauce and with a little bit of piccalilli was his normal diet. The insipid food of the nuns pleases him only partly. Yet it is better than the daily fear of whether or not those black scoundrels have poisoned his food. Now, he gets his meals from the nuns in a large tin box with a lock, for which only he and the nuns have a key.

Van Dam found the operation in a desolate state and, almost happy with the thievish acts of the Bakubas because they gave him a reason for his mistrust, he went to Father Vesteeg.

"Now you see it! These are those honest friends of yours! Those sensitive men of nature! Can you now ensure that I will get back two or three hundred scuffed planks, since they took away at least that many! And how will I get that old Ford back? And the parts of the drilling machine, the shovels, spades, and hammers? They simply stole sixty to seventy thousand francs worth from the company! And who is responsible for that? I am, of course. That will cause quite a stir in Matadi and Brussels when I report it! It will cost me my position! And they might make me pay for the damage!"

Versteeg understood. He felt caught between the two edges of sharp pincers. He knew all too well how little understanding the Bakubas have of "mine" and "yours," but he couldn't be harsh against these weaklings. Because … the example they see all the time isn't very uplifting. Doesn't Van Dam know how well the Negro population is aware of the fierce fighting between businesses for concessions? How well they know all about the cheating of the local directors of large plantations? How they know all about the mess caused by the representatives of important trading companies? On top of which, the task of the fifty years of missionary work for civilizing that population is a drop of clear water in the large bucket of gross, stinking wetness which the methods of colonization have poured over the Congo.

"I understand your difficult situation perfectly, Van Dam. But why not just go talk to Bolingé? Maybe the greater portion…"

"What? Are we really going to ask whether those dirty *macaques* would be so kind as to return all the stuff they had stolen? Versteeg, that's insane…"

"Then I will go talk with Bolingé myself about the matter. I believe everything will be put right."

The Bakubas did not abuse the trust of Father Versteeg. For one week, Van Dam found things back every morning at the concession, all the goods which had disappeared. Even the old Ford returned to its place in the warehouse. Versteeg never told him that the chassis and steering system had been thoroughly inspected at the trade school of the friars and that they had reassembled the whole thing. Two weeks after his discussion with Versteeg, Van Dam made an inventory. There were still about twenty planks missing, but he didn't think it was necessary to report that to the company.

The Bakubas' need is urgent. The missions help, but you can't maintain a population of twelve hundred souls, spread over eight villages, with canned food, nor keep it alive with imported edibles from Europe. The head of the White Fathers in Boma and the leaders of the other Orders in the Congo beg for help from the government, their Orders in Belgium, and the Flemish and Walloon people, and not without success. There is help, but the need remains, and becomes more urgent every week, every month. Pioneers like Versteeg understand how little that help means. They know that it isn't a temporary slump that could be combatted by makeshift measures. They know that the hopeless suffering of millions of Negroes is a curse to the colonial system of robbery, ignorance, and poor management. How often had these pioneers predicted what ended up happening. How intensely they protested against the removal of thousands of Negroes out of rich districts – where their primitive existence was assured – to the mines – where they now starved, unemployed, dejected, and listless. But these pioneers were only missionaries who knew their catechism. What did they know about colonial economics? Their voice sounded like crying in the wilderness.

At his simple writing table, Versteeg read a letter from the head office in Boma. Eighty cases of Portuguese sardines had been allotted to the mission. Eighty cases, Versteeg calculated, that would be three thousand eight hundred forty cans. If a Bakuba could live off just one can of sardines per day, then that shipment would mean three days of food for the population of Mta and the other villages in the district. Yes ... if! And even so ... only three days, what are three days in a long chain of bleak days, in an endless rosary of days with hunger? But Versteeg knew how complicated it was to provide even three days of food for his Bakubas, and he wrote a warm thank you to his provincial supervisor.

Adolf Verreet

Paternalistic Benevolence

Adolf Verreet (Turnhout 1894 – Mol 1950) was a missionary of the Order of Scheut. He left for the Congo in 1923, where he worked at different mission posts. Due to poor health, he had to return to Belgium in 1950, where he died in the same year. He published *Zwarte maatjes* (1932; Black Pals), a book for teenagers; *Het zwarte leven van Mabumba* (1935; The Black Life of Mabumba), a novel; and two autobiographical books: *Mijn klein, klein dorpke*... (1949; My Tiny, Tiny, Little Village) and *Onder de parasolboom* (1950; Underneath the Umbrella Tree).

Het zwarte leven van Mabumba describes the life of Mabumba, the chief of the Kumba village located on a tributary of the Congo River. The village is isolated, and people still follow old traditions. European civilization has not yet affected the lives of the villagers. Mabumba is married to Efonga, the daughter of Effindi, the chief of the neighboring Gwele tribe; his life becomes hell when Efonga runs away to Kinshasa and Effindi demands the return of their son, Elamba, or, in exchange for him, the two best fishing spots (*molukas*) of the Kumba. In desperation, Mabumba declares war on Effindi. The intervention of a missionary and the wise counsel of the district administrator prevent war from breaking out. After accepting the authority of the Europeans and welcoming Catholicism, Kumba undergoes a radical change. Civilization and new customs start to flourish. The unwavering belief of the Europeans in the superiority of Western culture and their firm conviction that they are the source of all wisdom result in a paternalistic attitude toward the African villagers.

The missionaries bring Western culture to the Congolese; however, they also want to shield them against the temptation of the unsavory aspects of European civilization, such as immorality. Even as they adopt the positive aspects of Western culture, Africans must remain simple, unspoiled children of nature; only then can they find happiness. Mabumba, who is baptized and lives a peaceful life in his small village, is the prototype of such a good African. In his village, the Catholic Mabumba is the happiest man in the world. He remarries and has two more children. Verreet's depiction of the ideal African who willingly subjects himself to the teachings of the missionaries, accepts the authority of the colonial state, and is satisfied with a tranquil existence in his village, fits perfectly into the Catholic and civil agenda.

Extract originally published as:

Verreet, A. *Het zwarte leven van Mabumba* (Leuven: Davidsfonds, 1935), 134–41.

Translated with permission from Standaard Uitgeverij.

The Black Life of Mabumba

"The white man? Which white man?"

"The white man who has come to our village … he has a long beard, father … see, there he is, he brought a lot of chests with him…"

Mabumba now saw a white figure in front of his hut, taller than the ring of black bodies which surrounded him. Strange men sat on the ground, resting from the journey and the hardships of carrying.

He came nearer and the circle of black men gave way for him.

"*Mbote*, man, what is your name?"

"My name is Mabumba and I am the chief of Kumba."

"Oh, well, chief, I was here years ago; at that time, I met another who was chief."

"Lipasa, yes, a brave man."

"So brave that he even refused to grant me hospitality and requested me to go stay at Effindi's place. I saw him, at least I believe, one more time, in Lie on the other shore of the river. He seemed much weaker at that time and had aged. That he is dead, now, what a shame! Because even Lipasa has a soul…"

"White man, Lipasa wasn't your enemy – when he died we found a medal on him, which your followers carry. And, therefore, I say to you as well: stay here at my hut … even though you come at a bad time."

"A bad time, Mabumba – why?"

"Why? The drums of war of Bondabure will soon announce it: the men of Kumba, we are at war with Effindi: I have declared it!"

The eyes opened wide and the mouths gaped with surprise.

"Effindi asked, no, demanded, one of two things: either the *molukas* of Bondabure and Mokori, or Elamba. I couldn't decide on one or the other, and said: 'I give you nothing, you hear, nothing, and take that as you like!' Then I fled back here. Men, have your spears and shields ready, and shelter the women in Mokori, near the grave of Lipasa: he will protect them. Where should we take shelter with Elamba?" The women ran around screaming and beat their breasts with their hands. The men went to their huts and took the spears and shields, which had not been used for many years, out of the joists of the roofs. Only Mopipo didn't get agitated and stared at the ground and shook his head: "Madness, Mabumba, madness!"

"What do you mean, madness? Go and get your spears, and help the women get away, before it gets dark."

"Madness, Mabumba. The time of war is over. If this had happened ten years ago, then this place would be red with our blood, and the last Kumba-man would lie rattling around in the mud. Don't worry, Effindi won't beat the war drums anymore: they would hear it in Lisala!"

"He can still abduct Elamba, forcefully."

"He won't."

"Then our *molukas* will still be taken away, our nets and dams destroyed, and he will establish his own fisheries there."

"Maybe. That's what it's all about, Mabumba: our fisheries; his desire for Elamba is merely a threat, a substitute; why don't you give him the boy and…"

"Mopipo!"

"And Effindi himself will send him back as a gift to you before eight days are over."

"Not for a day, not even for an hour will Elamba fall into his hands. I would rather strangle him with my own hands."

The white man, who had listened to the altercation and watched the strange behavior of the men and women, intervened and spoke:

"Mabumba, I am a guest of yours, and, therefore, the interests of your village are mine. Tell me what it's about… Look, those women there in the pirogues with packs and bags, have them come back, Mabumba! Make them wait, and call all your elders together so that we can have a debate and see what should be done." The women came back and squatted down near the pirogues, where they had piled up their packed possessions. The men all sat in a circle on wooden blocks or small stools.

Standing up, gesturing with hands and feet, his whole body mimicking his words, Mabumba now told the white man the circumstances of the affair. He went back to its deepest roots: from the crocodile, which took his fiancée, to his marriage with Effindi's daughter. Well into his speech, he involved his fellow villagers in his story by asking them: "Is it not true what I say?" after which all the heads then nodded, and all the mouths mumbled: "Yes, so it is, it isn't a lie, so it is."

Then he told what he had already suffered long ago, how hard he had worked after the birth of Elamba and, later, Efonga's flights to Molembi. All this to keep the greed of Effindi always satisfied, who even then already wanted to become master of the beautiful fisheries of Kumba: or isn't this what it is all about?

"That's what it was all about, of course."

So, they went to Lipasa on Mokori Island for advice with each new case, and he helped them and gave them a new perspective, a way out. Until he was found dead, on the same day Efonga had left with a boatswain from Lisala to go far away, downstream, where the large cities were. "Never have I asked for the money back which all of Kumba and I paid for Efonga, never. Because we knew that Efonga would come back, right?"

Now the choir's answer sounded curt and terse, and seemed purely a formality, but some mumbled as if in silence, "that's right."

Then at last this morning, the war had come, when Effindi himself repurchased his daughter and immediately demanded the child, or the fisheries of Bondabure and Mokori.

"And now, can we hand them the fisheries on which the Kumba have lived for as long as they have existed?"

"No, never," sounded from every mouth, with determination, while the men jumped up to give more emphasis to their words.

"Or will we let Elamba, the little boy of Kumba, be sent to Effindi, and let him be changed into a Gwele-kid?"

"Never, never, never." The heads shook powerfully at this answer and their hands turned into fists.

"You see, white man, what remains for us to do. And how you will find yourself in a battle which can't be postponed much longer."

The white man had listened with rapt attention and waited until all became silent and all eyes looked to him for advice. Then he cast his eyes down, and his lips moved without speaking. At last, he looked benignly at each of the men in the circle, and spoke:

"Mabumba, and all the elders of Kumba: I have heard your case, a great debate, a complex conflict…"

"A complex conflict, *bongo*, that it is."

"It is clear that this conflict can't be resolved any longer with a war, as you would have done twenty years ago: God forbids it, and the State will prevent it. A conflict like this must be resolved between the two parties. Allow me therefore to send someone to Effindi, and to invite him to come here. If the circumstances of the affair are as you have explained, then, it seems to me, the outcome is clear: Effindi will keep his money, and you your child and your *molukas*."

"That is how it must be! That way – and no other!"

"However, Mabumba and Kumba people, it would have been so much easier if Efonga had remained with her husband and child. If the wife had loved the husband, and he the wife, those two hearts would have become one, unbreakably one! If all the people had accepted that one shouldn't take away someone else's wife or child or goods, they would not have even desired it in the depths of their hearts! If everyone saw that you can put away all the spears and shields for good, as soon as you learn to respect God's commandments…"

Now only a sigh could be heard, and the silence of the men revealed their agreement in the depths of their souls.

"Had Efonga known God's law, that the woman cannot leave her husband, and had Effindi known God's other law, that one cannot covet the goods of one's neighbors, and had you all, Gweles and Kumbas, respected God's commandments: all men are children of the same God, so as brothers of each other, they must love and help and assist each other. Because what you have done to the least of men, you have done to

God himself. Had all those words lived in your hearts, men of Kumba, tell me, would so much blood have flowed in this area, and would the war shields still have been dragged out of the huts today for a new war?"

They all sat there, dead quiet, with bowed heads. Then, Mabumba stood up and spoke:

"White man, I want to know the laws of God; teach them to me" and many eyes turned to him, and said silently: "Me too – teach them to me!"

"I want to force no one. Let he who wants to hear the teachings of God stand up and say his name. I came here years ago with the same goal, to preach God's word to you, and since you didn't want to hear it, I left. Now I have come back and l leave it up to you to decide what to do."

"White man," Mopipo spoke, "I don't want it, because you want to take away our children. That is why Lipasa refused before, and that is also the reason why I still refuse today."

"Not one of your children will ever see the village of the white men, unless he asks for it himself … understood? A teacher, a black man like you, who has learned all the laws and words of God, will come to live here in Kumba. He will teach you daily, and there will come a day when you will feast and dance to commemorate what happened here today. Build a hut for your teacher – whom we call a catechist – and before the week ends he will come here, okay?"

"White man of God," Mabumba spoke, "you yourself stay with us!"

"Impossible, children! I have to visit other villages, where many live who already have become children of God. Still I will return, that is certain."

The white man had now taken a book and asked with his eyes who would say his name.

"I, Mabumba."

"And I, Angondo, and there my wife Nzali: she must!"

"And I … and I …" and so twenty names were written in the Father's book. Others still hesitated, and finally agreed with Mopipo when he said:

"There is no rush; we will first think about building a new hut."

"So, it is understood then: you will build a house for the catechist here, in the middle of the village, and help him initially with some food. You will come daily to listen to his lessons and then you remain free to do what you think best. Is that good?"

Bert Nacht

No Place like Home

Bert Nacht is the pseudonym of B. Nuyts. The short story "De kerstnacht van Baliongo" (Baliongo's Christmas Night) originally appeared in the 1949 Christmas issue of *Band*, a cultural periodical that aimed to establish a bond between Flemings living in the Congo. The first issue was published in May 1942, a time when World War II had cut all contact between the colony and the mother country. Later, the short story was also excerpted in *Kongo ya lobi* (The Congo of Yesterday), for what should have been a jubilee edition of the periodical *Band* with selected short stories. The collection appeared in 1961, a year after the Belgian colony was granted its independence. The colonial period was over for good, and both the rule of the colonizers and the dominance of Western culture had come to an abrupt and unexpected end. The Belgian Congo had indeed become "The Congo of Yesterday."

Kongo ya lobi offers a sample of Flemish colonialist literature, in which the colonial mentality is still predominantly present. Recurring topics include the "boys" with their slyness and deceitfulness, the solidity of an old plantation owner, the nostalgic longing for faraway Flanders, as well as the unfathomability and naivety of the Congolese in contrast to the wisdom, magnanimity, and benevolence of the Belgian colonizers.

Nacht's story centers on Baliongo, a policeman in a small village who does not want to subject himself to the traditions of his tribe. His big dream is to visit Belgium one day. At the missionary school he attended, he was once given a calendar picture showing Antwerp's beautiful cathedral. He starts collecting all the pictures he can lay his hands on. For Baliongo, Belgium is the Promised Land. He succeeds in signing up as a sailor on a Congo boat, which arrives in Antwerp on Christmas Eve. But his dream clashes immediately with reality. He is not prepared for the cold; moreover, the hectic city overwhelms him. When Baliongo visits a pub together with his fellow sailors and a waitress wants to dance with him, he is panic-stricken and flees. Confused, he drifts through the streets of Antwerp until, by coincidence, he finds himself at the cathedral at the moment when midnight mass begins. Baliongo joins the congregation and realizes during the service that Belgium does not correspond to his ideal; he prays fervently to be allowed to return to his native village in the Congo.

"De kerstnacht van Baliongo" depicts Baliongo as a simple soul who can only find happiness in his traditional community. He does not belong in this city, in a country full of white people. This short story unintentionally lays bare the ambiguity at the basis of Belgian colonialism. On the one hand, the Congolese have to be converted and civilized, while, on the other hand, Western society remains alien and even frightening to them. They do not feel at home in this confusing and complex civilized world. For Nacht, the civilization of the Congolese has limits that should not be transgressed. Baliongo is Nacht's mouthpiece; his maladjustment to Western society is presented as a natural reaction for a primitive person. The story is, however, a blatant misrepresentation of the voice of the Congolese by the author who, through Baliongo, imposes his own colonial ideology on them.

> **Extract originally published as:**
> Nacht, B. *De kerstnacht van Baliongo* (1949), in: *Kongo ya lobi* (Leuven: Davidsfonds, 1961), 214–20.
> Translated with permission from Standaard Uitgeverij.

The Christmas Night of Baliongo

And so, he approaches the Promised Land.

Baliongo shivers as the ice-cold water from the hose sprays against his bare legs and feet. He has to clean the iron floor of the ship with a few other sailor boys because, tomorrow, they will all arrive in the large city of the white people. Baliongo is sick from the cold; it is the twelfth month, called December by the white people. Earlier, they certainly had told him that it could be very cold in that far-away land, especially when Christmas is celebrated. But he hadn't imagined it could be so harsh. The fathers had once given him a photo with a nativity scene in a white field. Baliongo thought at first that it was salt, or maybe flour, but the priest had told him it was water, water that had become hard from the cold just like in the ice-box at the mission. Baliongo thinks about all that while he jumps to and fro at a mad speed over the steel bolts on deck and waves his arms to get warm.

His comrades are very surprised that he doesn't have long pants and a heavy coat to ward off the cold and wind. Baliongo had never thought of that, and he immediately buys a dark blue suit from one of the sailor boys. They also want to sell him a shirt, but Baliongo refuses, because he has barely any money left. They laugh at the idiot and ask what he wants to do in "Antwerp," or whether he is maybe going to stay in his room during all the days that they are in the harbor. This is exactly what he doesn't want to do. And they whisper with the most serious faces: "If you want to walk around in the city, you must be dressed like a white man." Baliongo feels intimidated, since those men had already been in that country so often and knew a lot about it. So, he buys a shirt as white as sugar and a tie, shoes, and socks. There is only a tiny amount of francs left from the three years that he had worked as a police officer in the village by the river. They also tell him that he doesn't know enough French to go to the large city. When he hears all of this, Baliongo gets worried and desperate; he also can't ignore everything going on around him any longer: above him, the great masters, and, next to him, his black brothers, who recount strange things, adventures and experiences from their earlier visits to the land of the white men. He doesn't understand a lot of it and that night, he stays up longer than usual in his small alcove, brooding and lost in his thoughts. At least until once again he manages to bring order to his dreams: he has come here to see the promised land and its wonders and not to live there with those people.

The next morning, the first thing he does is ask his comrades what happens with the sailor boys who don't go back with their ship to Africa, who want to stay in the land of the white people. Many have tried, he receives as an answer, but they don't get far. In Belgium, there is no bush or savannah in which to hide. The entire country is one large city, where they notice you at once. You are sent back to Matadi on the first boat … and then what?

Then I would have seen the country, Baliongo thinks to himself, and what happens afterwards isn't really important.

Already he is snatched away from those new thoughts because it becomes busier on the ship. The gray water isn't so choppy anymore, and along the railing, the crew members stand in groups next to each other and point to the brown line of the riverbank with their index fingers. Now the miracle is going to happen, Baliongo thinks, and he waits ... all the interest is drawn to the other side, where, out of the gray mist, a brown silhouette appears: Antwerp. Baliongo's eyes cling to that faraway vision. Slowly everything becomes clearer; the shores come closer and enclose the water along all sides. The ship emits three prolonged blasts in the winter sky, and the echoing answers of boats large and small resound all around. The brown silhouette of the city is now close; houses, roofs, and walls, and streets are clearly visible. And there, on top of it all, is the tower of Our Lady's Cathedral. Baliongo smiles, a quiet silly smile of happiness: there is the tower and the church, the same one from the prayer card that he got from the priests. By my mother, he sighs, that is the tower and the church. His desires have become fulfilled.

Now things grow hectic, and Baliongo is no longer himself in this flurry. Everyone runs around, many tasks need to be taken care of, and he knows precisely what to do. Most of the sailor boys already have their best clothes on, with their white shirts and colorful ties. Baliongo also gets dressed. The boat is now against the quay wall; the white people go ashore, and others return to the ship. There are suitcases and luggage to be carried away. And after a couple of hours everything is quiet again. There is no more work to be done and the unloading hasn't even started, since tomorrow is Christmas and everyone gets the day off. The sailor boys form their own group and step ashore. Baliongo is with them. They walk along an endless series of large stone houses, which, for Baliongo, climb awfully high in the darkness of the winter evening. His friends know their way well in that forest of houses and buildings, and they feel at home. They enter a street where it is much busier. There are white people everywhere. It is now completely dark and, out of thousands of windows, lights shine red, white and pink, like a sinking sun in the mist. On top of a high building, advertising lights flash, and Baliongo looks with an open mouth at those silent lights that run along the houses and don't burn.

Suddenly the group goes inside a house. Baliongo follows because he doesn't know what else to do and clings, scared, to this last piece of familiarity: his own people. They come into a large room where lamps burn on all sides, with many tables, chairs, and white people. Baliongo wonders for a second whether they are allowed to be here in this place and walk freely between these important people. Then, they all sit down, the whole gang. A white lady comes and asks what they want to drink. As if in a feverish dream, Baliongo sees it all happen. The white lady comes back with a couple of glasses and bottles full of beer, which are immediately drunk and refilled. White people enter, and others leave. A couple of people go to the back of the hall where there is a podium. They start making music with all kinds of instruments. "When will our Congolese dance a Negro dance?" someone shouts. Some of his friends jump up and, while the white people on the podium start making a devilish noise, they jump around, pull faces and call out crazy things in their native tongue. All the white people take great pleasure in these foolish antics and laugh aloud while pounding the tables with their fists, so that the beer jumps up in the glasses. When his friends get tired, and the musicians as well, they return to their table, shining with pleasure and asking for beer, more beer. Later in the evening, a different kind of people come, bringing a different type of joy. Now, there is dancing, white women and men who don't dance alone like Baliongo's brothers and sisters do in the moonlit night in the village by the large river. The white people dance in pairs, man and woman, close to each other, and without singing or shouting. Baliongo suddenly notices one of the ship boys dancing with a white lady, the one who brought them beer earlier.

Baliongo is shocked; an inexplicable fear comes over him. He feels something around him, without seeing it, a dark impending disaster. He fears death because he doesn't understand this life.

The white lady is back again; she doesn't bring beer but she doesn't take any glasses away. She comes to Baliongo, smiles at him, stands next to him and asks him something he doesn't understand. She smiles again, sits very close to him to whisper something in his ear. Her warm breath blows over his cheeks, and there is a scent of strange flowers. She takes him by his arm, and his hand, and begins to count his fingers.

At that moment, Baliongo sees the sorcerer in the moonlight throw his shimmering stones of fate. He looks for the man who called the crocodiles out of the river and to the yellow shore in order to have them drag two children away. The sorcerer picks up the stones again and points at Baliongo.

The white lady has counted the fingers of both his hands now and lays her head on his shoulders.

Baliongo cannot stand it anymore and looks for the door.

He wants to flee, far away from this incomprehensible situation. But what if the white people jump on him to keep him here? To force him to stay? Then he would fight … but against whom? Not against a white person. Slowly he stands up and goes to the door. No one looks at him. When he goes outside, he shivers from the biting cold and wind. People come and go, appearing out of the darkness on one side and disappearing into the darkness on the other. No one remains standing there as Baliongo does, so he too leaves, without knowing where to go. At the street corner he bumps into a couple of white people, who say something in Flemish that he doesn't understand: "verdomde neger" [stupid Negro].

Baliongo, the stupid Negro.

And then he hears the voice of the sorcerer again: "You can't walk away, not to the priests, not to the mission, you have to pay for the kids who were taken away by the crocodile."

He walks on the dark side of the street, avoiding the light, until he suddenly comes to an open area. There, in the dark misty air, a tower of stone rises up before him. He doesn't want to look at it out of fear of a new disillusionment and turns around. How cold it is in this place, where the wind is so sharp and wild. And Baliongo thinks of the small village by the river, where the sun is so nice and warm. He wants to go back. He starts to walk; he needs to go back to the ship, back to the sea, home. He hears hasty steps behind him; those were surely the white people who were following and wanted to drag him with them. He walks faster, like a hunted antelope. He runs until he can't any longer, and stands somewhere in a dark corner, panting from exhaustion. He has lost his way in between all those streets and houses and dark alleys.

Something falls on his forehead, soft, and a drop of water leaks over his face. In the yellow light of a faraway lamp he sees thousands of grey crumbs fall softly to the ground, like leaves off a tree. Around him all these wondrous things fall. That must be snow. His face and hands become wet and chilly. He undoes his tie and dries his face with it. He wants to go back to the water to search for the ship, and, without knowing it, he follows the silent people, who all are going in the same direction. Then, he arrives back at the church. He doesn't see the tower anymore; everything disappears in the fuzzy rain of flakes. The snow starts falling heavier and heavier around him, and, when he tries to catch a flake in his hands, he only finds a drop of water. From all sides, people come and enter that great church. And Baliongo goes along.

At the back of the endless building, where the shadows are the darkest, Baliongo goes and hides himself. After he manages to recover a little, he starts to look around from his hidden corner. There are empty chairs around him, white men come inside and sit down, statues are everywhere on the walls, and over there... is the altar. It is a thousand times more beautiful in the shine of gold and light, a thousand times more beautiful than the one in the small church of the mission in his village. But it is the same altar, where the same Lord lives. And Baliongo feels a blessed peace come over him. Here, he feels at home, here there are no men to bother him and ask him things he can't do. Here everyone is in silent contemplation, facing the altar peacefully.

The silver bell of the altar rings, and the midnight mass begins. Baliongo raises the legs of his pants and places his bare knees on the hard wood of the chair, until they hurt. And while somewhere high in the church children's voices sing *Gloria in excelsis Deo*, Baliongo prays "Lord, let me forget everything that has happened here today. That wasn't for me. I want to go back to my village by the river, to the mission. Help me and give me peace." High under the vaults it echoes: *Et in terra pax hominibus bonae voluntatis.*

Alfons Walschap

Inner Conflict

Alfons Walschap (Londerzeel 1903 – Antwerp 1938) was brother to the famous author Gerard Walschap. As a missionary in the Congregation of the Missionaries of the Sacred Heart of Jesus, he was sent to the mission of Coquilhatville (present-day Mbandaka) in 1932. He lived in Boende, Boteka, and Bolima before returning to Belgium in 1938. Gravely ill, he died that same year.

Walschap's scant work is characterized by immersion in the lives of the Africans. He empathizes with the Congolese and tries to understand them by studying their culture. He is acutely aware of the divide between white and black and the disorienting impact of the presence of the colonizer and the missionary on the Congolese and their societies. In a letter to a fellow missionary, he makes the following self-critical remark: "We have already destroyed so many people but done very little which suits these people. We have made trousers for them that are much too big, and now they get lost in them. We have fished with baskets without bottoms, and some are surprised that the fish have fallen through. I intuitively understand the situation much better than I can express. The people escape us. And nevertheless we have to carry on, you in the city and I here with a people that is dying out."

In addition to serving as a missionary, Walschap was also a composer of Congolese church music and a writer. Apart from a limited number of poems and seventeen Congolese dirges, he wrote three prose texts: the short story "Longwangu de smid" (Longwangu the Blacksmith), a literary fragment called "Bolalimai," and three instalments of "De ring sluit toe" (The Ring Closes), a preliminary study for a novel.

Walschap makes the Congolese central characters in his texts and tries to understand their minds. In "Longwangu de smid," Longwangu's inner conflict – he has to give up his tribal traditions and long-held beliefs in order to become a Christian – forms the core of the short story. Ultimately, Longwangu decides to be baptized. The personal struggle of the fictional protagonist with the expectations of his tribe and his difficulties with abandoning polygamy make the draw of Christianity appear very powerful in this conversion story.

> **Extract originally published as:**
> Walschap, A. *Longwangu de smid*, in: *Het letterkundig werk van Alfons Walschap*, intr. Vital Celen (Antwerp: De Sikkel, 1952), 115–21.

── Longwangu the Blacksmith

In his dream, Longwangu is carried to the source of the blacksmiths. He is seized by a great fear. The source suddenly becomes agitated and emits pitch-black smoke, out of which Nkema, Father of all forging, steps forth. He touches Longwangu and says: "My son, do what your spirit tells you." Longwangu wakes up, drenched in sweat.

The woman asks: "Are you sick, Longwangu?"

He tells her his dream.

She says: "You want to leave us, you want to be baptized."

He replies: "Be quiet, that's ridiculous."

Be quiet – he said, but what she said earlier was true, only he doesn't dare to acknowledge it; maybe he doesn't dare to believe it himself. He cannot believe how it is possible that this is happening to him. And he starts to wait for what is going to come, or what he thinks must inevitably come. Because it is clear to him that a destiny has been allotted for him, a destiny he can't escape from any longer. The punishment which has pushed him down for so long, the arrival of the priest, the words which he learned from the mouth of his ancestor, spoken to him in a dream – all of this has been planned by the almighty, to get him where the almighty wants him.

He will do what his spirit tells him to do, and nothing else.

Time passes by, and he starts to long intensely for the priest and his baptism. At the same time, he is scared that the priest will stand next to him in the blacksmith shop again at any moment and warmly greet him.

Longwangu imagines how he would then have to make an effort to say that he wishes to stick to that new teaching, and that he wishes to be baptized. How the priest would once again confront him concerning the teaching about marriage, and how he then would have to send away his four other wives. But how or whether all of this could possibly come to be, how or whether this could all really happen – no, he cannot imagine that.

And the people, what will they say then?

The people.

Those people don't wait until it happens, not usually. People always anticipate events in their gossip. People generally don't have so much patience.

They already mock him enough.

And his wives?

They cheat on him.

He had neglected them so much recently that it took a long time before he was aware of their behavior. Of course, he would now kill and fight; he would first act as if nothing was going on, but would catch them red-handed one night or another, stab their lovers, and the wives themselves – oh, they know what was in store for them.

But he keeps pretending that nothing is wrong; he keeps avoiding catching them in the act. In his mind he hears a very weak voice tell him, let them search, Longwangu, let them search, maybe their lovers will come to you to buy them.

Longwangu does what his mind tells him, with the faint hope that this will make things easier.

Later he still gets jealous again.

What does he do?

Get a knife, a spear, a club? Nothing of the sort.

He calls his wives to him, all five, and tells them what is happening among them and that he knows everything.

And now Longwangu shows that he is starting to lose his mind; he educates his wives, he teaches them.

If your wife is unfaithful, do you strike her lover down, punish her in the way our forefathers have designed?

No.

Longwangu teaches his wives a lesson.

The women, of course, spread the news, and the harsh mocking becomes rampant.

Doesn't that hurt him? It hurts him deeply, it causes him deep sorrow, but Longwangu follows the voice of his spirit, his timid and humiliated spirit, but he doesn't dare be disobedient to the voice.

He calls the women to him again.

Longwangu goes to great lengths.

"There are two types of sorrow," he says as he stands in front of them. "The first kindles anger in you, the second oppresses your mind."

"The sadness that you have caused me at present belongs to the second type," he explains extensively.

He ends with the following words:

"See, I have treated you with kindness, and you who have cheated on me have exposed me to the general mockery of people."

"Do what your spirit tells you," he says.

The women left.

Did Longwangu really mean to teach his women so seriously, or had he become a coward? This is what people were now wondering about – in any case, he achieved the opposite with his wives.

A woman will lay out her ruses, all her cunning during the day to cheat on her man, but will not let any sign of a cooling down on his part go unavenged.

The wives of Longwangu couldn't stand it anymore, to be so neglected by him. On the days they were supposed to do the work for him, they refused to prepare food, or to bring him water – in short, to do for him what a Negro woman must do and perform for her lord and master. They also acted in this way because they themselves had become victims of the mocking in the village about Longwangu, especially among the other women of the tribe.

They were constantly reproached because they belonged to a man who didn't desire them anymore.

Could anyone insult a woman more deeply and coarsely?

You couldn't, and, yes, they fought against it and threatened to flee from Longwangu.

Did Longwangu keep them in chains? They could go where they wanted to go. He had long since made clear that they must do what their spirits told them to do; yes, that's what they had to do.

Is that an answer?

It isn't an answer.

The women stayed.

But now the family members of the wives approach him and ask Longwangu what he intended to do with his wives.

Longwangu says that there was nothing that he intended to do with them – nothing that he was not permitted to do. Or did they mean that he didn't know what he was supposed to do as far as the women were concerned?

"I have paid a dowry for all these women. If another man is found who desires to take one of these women as his wife, let him take her, as long as he brings me a dowry, as long as he pays for her."

Longwangu had come to a point that he announced this in public to the families of his wives.

But now that he acknowledged it, the women didn't want to lose him. They had been the wives of the most prominent man in the tribe. They were getting old, and they secretly went so far as to beg Longwangu to let them stay. Jealous of each other, they competed in serving him in the best possible way, in order to find mercy in his eyes.

In this way, Longwangu saw when he talked in front of the family members of his wives that he had achieved the opposite effect of what he had intended.

Because of the wives, the family members started to flatter and grovel in order to outdo other family members. Nothing motivates like jealousy. The entire tribe is involved in it.

Longwangu finds himself in the middle of all this. He does not know any more what he should or should not do. He feels that he is acting in a way that people thought was ridiculous, that, as far as his wives were concerned, he had let things go too far. They are, after all, his property and as far as the people are concerned, oh well.

And then the priest appears.

Greetings.

"Where is Joannes?" Longwangu asks.

"Joannes has no time now. He is traveling around and preparing people here and there for holy baptism. In other villages there are so many people who wish to be baptized."

And look, now, the moment of speaking has come for Longwangu, but the priest has so little time, and he wants to get going right away because he still has to go far today.

Longwangu doesn't dare to be honest about his desire, even more so because so many people came to listen, for everyone thought that Longwangu would now speak.

Longwangu had also thought so, but he didn't dare to.

He decided to wait for Joannes.

The priest leaves immediately.

Longwangu is alone again.

Now the ridicule knows no boundaries.

He is despised; he is not a man.

And yet Longwangu keeps waiting until the inevitable does come.

After a long time, Joannes finally comes, and Longwangu can speak freely. Joannes is happy to be able to help him.

During the preparations for Longwangu, there is enough time to settle the situation with the women, and, on a beautiful day, the priest comes and baptizes him together with his first wife.

Gerard Walschap

A Humane Approach to Colonization

Considered one of the most influential Flemish writers of the twentieth century, Gerard Walschap (Londerzeel 1898 – Antwerp 1989) wrote poetry, essays, plays, and prose. *Houtekiet* (1939) is arguably his most important novel. Walschap undertook a journey through the Congo from the end of March to mid-June 1951, at the invitation of the Belgian Ministry of the Colonies. Even before his arrival in the colony, he planned on using his experience as the basis for a novel. Upon his return, he started writing *Oproer in Congo* (1953; Rebellion in the Congo). The novel was well received and was awarded the triennial prize for colonial literature.

Oproer in Congo deals with a rebellion against Michel van Aspengouwen, a well-to-do plantation owner. After the murder of a missionary, Van Aspengouwen organizes a manhunt to find the perpetrator. Under the leadership of the *évolué* Johannes, the local population rebels against Van Aspengouwen's disproportionate use of violence. The rebels round up the whites and imprison them in the local church. There, long-winded discussions take place between the whites and the blacks. Johannes speaks about the merits of colonization. After Johannes and his fellow blacks are allowed to regain their dignity, they set the Belgians free.

The novel highlights a cross section of colonial society in which the rich plantation owner, the missionary, and the *évolué* are the main antagonists. In the selected extract, each of them gets the opportunity to present his point of view. The rebellion ends without bloodshed, but the relationship between Africans and Europeans is put on a new footing. The exploitation of the Congo is rejected. Van Aspengouwen has to return to Belgium. He is replaced by his son, who believes in a new approach. Johannes is promoted to supervisor of the workforce.

In *Oproer in Congo*, Walschap does not criticize colonization itself, but the way in which it is implemented. The solution he proposes calls for respect for the Africans. The unequivocal message of the novel is that a different attitude toward the Congolese people is imperative. Although the novel takes a critical look at colonization, it still clings to the idea of the surplus value of Western civilization and the necessity for Africans to adopt it. By doing so, the novel underwrites the Belgian colonial ethos and even provides a legitimization for it. Indeed, the call for a colonization with a human touch does not intrinsically alter the balance of power between black and white.

> **Extract originally published as:**
> Walschap, G. *Oproer in Congo* (Amsterdam: Elsevier, 1953), 180–89. Translated with permission from Standaard Uitgeverij.

Rebellion in the Congo

Johannes still had a lot more to say. He had to apologize for being unable to explain better the opinions and questions from his extensive thinking and reading. His mind was torn apart. When he was in the church, his mind was elsewhere, but, when he was elsewhere, his mind was in the church. Among the people in front of the church were men from the surrounding regions who had brought along weapons. No one knew why they had come or who had asked them. When the people had broken up on his command, these men had left to go to the trading post, which wasn't on their way. Makondo had not wanted to threaten them with his armed men but used a good ruse by letting Mombita silently walk around them. They didn't know that Mombita had no power anymore and had left in what seemed like a friendly way. When Makondo told this to Johannes, to find out if those men were friends or foes and if he should chase them, Johannes couldn't think because he remembered his discussion with the white people, and now that he was in conversation with the white people, he thought that this could perhaps be a ruse and that those men had been asked to apprehend him. His heart felt torn apart too. When he listened to the white men, he trusted them, but when he thought about those men, he distrusted them.

The bishop stood up and spoke in a serious manner: "Johannes, the Belgian authorities will learn what happened here and will intervene. We don't know what they will do. We here in the church didn't call those black men, we are not setting up a trap for you."

It surprised the white men that Johannes didn't respond to this announcement, but they forgot it, captivated by what he said.

"Mr. Beddegenoot has made me understand why the white men should and could come here. I can accept that view if the white men understand that this does not allow them to act as rulers. They are strangers in a land that they took with violence and must win with friendship."

"Exactly, Johannes, that is what I meant."

"The white man gives the black man two bitter pills: learning and working. He doesn't want to swallow them, but the white man treats him like a child that is sick and doesn't want bitter medicine. He says: you want to become civilized, then you also have to learn and work. But is that everything the white man does?

He takes away gold, diamonds, copper, and tin from the Congo; he takes away what grows on our soil. The plantations were developed by the white men; they hold their value, they make our country richer. But the diamonds, gold, copper, and tin don't increase any more. By and large, the Congolese work to make their land poorer and the white men richer. They dig up a hundred francs, and they get ten. Look, says the white man, how rich the work makes you; you didn't have those ten francs earlier. But before they came, the black man had a hundred. Sure, they were in the ground, he didn't know about it and he couldn't get to it. But when the country is once again his, when he can run it, he will have become ninety francs poorer for every ten francs earned from the white man."

All four white men, Beddegenoot, Dr. Persoons, the Monsignor, and Father Edward raised their fingers, as if in class. Johannes wanted to continue talking. The four couldn't keep quiet, started, stopped with a polite apology, made an inviting gesture to let each other talk first. Father Rik interrupted. He lowered the four fingers with a wide wave and gave a tap on Johannes' shoulder with his bony index finger to let him know that he could continue to speak. He snapped his head backwards a couple of times, while his long beard waved like the tail of a Shetland pony, as if to say "Just wait, now it's going to come." And it came. He listened with his eyes pointed to the ceiling, as if he was hearing heavenly music. The outstretched arm with the vertical index finger fell on Johannes from time to time, confirming how true his words were and how well-spoken they were.

"Regarding that ten francs profit with a loss of ninety," Johannes said, "losing what one can't use is not terrible. But, in addition, the black man loses everything he possesses. It was nothing in your eyes, but everything in his, and the father said that this was also part of becoming civilized. He lived in small villages that were large families. Many villages together, that lived in friendship and intermarried, formed a tribe. Each village lived off its own soil; the black man was a small landowner, a free farmer. The white man made him into a servant. The black man who dares to approach you to take part in your civilization loses his freedom and independence; he becomes a servant. A servant in your villa, a servant on your plantation, a servant in your factory, a servant in your mine. A proletarian. If he could have chosen freely, he could have blamed himself, but he was forced to do so. Many white men get rich by dragging the black people out of their villages to the factory and mine. What are those?"

"Slave traders," said Father Rik, with his eyes to the ceiling, and his finger fell again, a signal to continue.

"How many black people," asked Johannes, "are really in the voluntary service of white people?"

"Not a single one," said Father Rik and gave a new signal.

"If I think about it, white men, I wonder sometimes what you have actually done here: did you bring a civilization or did you destroy one?"

"Destroyed," said Father Rik.

His fellow priests started to become uncomfortable with the discussion. The Monsignor murmured to Father Edward: "I wonder if he will now start to talk about the Twelve Apostles too? As soon as Rik starts ranting about the Congo, he always brings up the argument that there aren't too few, but far too many missionaries because Christ converted the entire world with only twelve apostles." In his turn, Father Edward whispered excuses about his colleague to Dr. Persoons and Beddegenoot. "He's had amebic dysentery for twenty years now," he whispered, "and you know better than I do how amoebas generate abscesses in the lungs, liver, and brain. We had a brother who went insane from it. We fear that it will be the same with him. He is a wise man, full of character, a good person through and through. The Monsignor always says: an angel in the guise of a pirate, but bordering on foolishness. For example, he once, in all seriousness, proposed a detailed plan to divide the Congo in two halves between Wallonia and Flanders. He claimed that Walloons were not able to colonize, whereas the Flemish were the best colonizers in the world. In the Congo, the Flemish should get the chance to show what they can do without the Walloons spoiling their work. Every Belgian city and village should adopt a Congolese city or village and send emigrants there. He said that our colonization is too much exploitation and too little interpenetration. He wanted to let young farmers, workmen and craftsmen from his village in West Flanders come to his missionary village and establish themselves with their own means, without help from the government. At that point, the bishop called him to the vicariate. The State officials, Rik had argued, humiliate and rebuff the black people; the industrialists proletarianize them; the common man, however, is the true, natural civilizer who can adapt and can lift the natives to a level they can reach. We tell him then to look at South Africa, but then he answers: 'those are Dutch Protestants'."

"Yes, yes," murmured the doctor, "the Flemish are God's chosen people, the abscesses are in his brain, father."

"He is a good person, doctor, a good person through and through; I don't say it to mock him."

"Nor do I; I'm proposing a diagnosis."

There was no reaction from the Monsignor, Edward, Beddegenoot, and the doctor, but from Celestin, who until then had not said a single word. He suddenly became furious. The mission had always supported his father, who was the biggest exploiter of the Congo, but now he saw to his annoyance that the one who rebelled against his father was unconditionally supported by a missionary.

"If the whites messed it up here," he claimed," then you bear the most responsibility, because you have been here the longest." His finger pointed right in the face of Father Rik. "And if the black people should own land, why did you forbid them to take a second wife to work the soil?"

Johannes' mind became a cave full of rebounding echoes. Monsieur Celestin had lifted his head, had spoken, to show that he still existed. Father Rik watched Celestin from under the scrubland of his eyebrows, reckoning whether he should eat up, blow away, ignore, or laugh at that little man. The Monsignor took Father Rik by the arm and led him away, out of fear that he would blame the missionaries for everything and would start talking about the twelve apostles, or would argue against the collection of used postage stamps for the missions, another one of his favorite topics. Did Saint Paul live off postage stamps? Saint Paul earned his bread with weaving and converted the whole world, so we have to work. Rik resisted, but the Monsignor persevered softly, powerfully, and in a kindly manner and got him to the sacristy for a visit to the sick. Father Edward now pleaded vigorously with Celestin and Johannes for his good colleague with peculiar views which were not shared by the other missionaries. Then everything fell silent and the small and dynamic Beddegenoot, who had comforted himself with a library for his failed career, stood up with self-satisfaction.

"Johannes, it is a pleasure to talk to you. I don't know too many white men with whom one can have a discussion like this. When this adventure is behind us, I invite you to come to my house; my library is at your service. You are well on your way, but you must go further.

Ask a white man why he has come here, and he will say this: to bring civilization. That is not a lie, but it is an easy and harmonious formula because it isn't possible to fully answer this question. Don't take it literally. Because if you go to a mine of *Union Minière*, or to a plantation of *Cultures du Congo* and you wonder whether they are bringing civilization, colonization looks like hypocrisy. It is easy to stir people up against us, but that is actually criminal and dumb.

See the things as they really are. Our king, Leopold II, says that all European countries had colonies, which made them rich, and that Belgium without a colony would stay poor and weak. He sought an area that hadn't been occupied by another country and found the Congo. Was he thinking about civilization? Well, no; he thought about Belgium. Did he think about you? No. He would have done nothing for you if it hadn't been beneficial for Belgium. For a long time, the Belgians didn't want his Congo, because they feared that it would cost them more than it would bring in. Was his civilization then a lie? No. He was strongly convinced that its colonization – with schools, missions, roads, plantations, factories, mines, and trade – would be of immeasurable benefit to you and that you couldn't resent us for our profit because yours was always larger. We, too, think so; it is, in fact, completely true, as you also will soon see.

Some white people say that colonization is a disaster for you. Others say that this is of no importance as long as the Congo keeps generating profits for them. The communists want to civilize you, but in their own way. If we do it, they call it exploitation. And there are still Africans who want to go back to their old civilization because they don't like ours.

That is all stupid, Johannes. We take away your ore and diamonds, yes, but you have enough of it for several centuries and, without us, you wouldn't have found them or been able to dig them up. We give you ten francs for every hundred in ore, but have you paid with those ten francs for the schools, churches, hospitals, factories, machines, villas, roads, cars, trains, and boats which will still stay in your country? No; we paid for those with the remaining ninety. The ore we took is of no use to you, but from what we gave you instead, you became a modern, civilized people. Development, the healing of your illnesses, the care for your children, welfare, comfort – are those not worth the ninety francs which were in the ground without your knowing?

The Congo must generate more, but your happiness is just as important to us because without it, we can't stay here, and we need to stay in order to make a profit. Coming here, starting here, is nothing other than a loss. It is not a question of humanity. If we can't gain your land and if we can't get you on our side, then we invested our capital poorly. In a word: your happiness is ours and your interests are ours.

The *evolué* says that the black man does the same work as the white man but gets only half of his pay. For starters, the black person works less hard and is less efficient. He works in his own climate while the white man works in a strange climate he can't bear. The black person has fewer needs. The industry in which he works costs more because everything must be exported, because he doesn't buy any of it himself, while the white man, with his salary, buys the products which he himself has made. If we gave the black mine worker in the Congo the same salary as the white mine worker in Belgium, the mines would go bankrupt. Do you really think that the white man gets his higher salary because he is seen as more human and the black man gets his lower salary because we don't like him? No, the white man had to fight for each franc of his salary, and it was given to him because he made it possible for it to be paid with his own work. You, too, will fight for every franc of your salary, and it will be given to you if you make it possible yourself.

The communist says that we first send a priest to subdue you and then a company to make you work. But what does he do himself? He first sends you a propagandist to stir you up against us, and, after you revolt against us, he will make you work harder than we do, and for even lower salaries.

And the old, lazy black man, Johannes, who mourns for his old civilization – how stupid. In this way, the old pagans mourned when Christianity was first preached to them; so did Christians mourn when their religion was torn apart, so do they mourn now because Christianity is in crisis, so people mourn wherever a new civilization breaks through. We found you here as small farmers, fishermen, and hunters. Meanwhile, new classes of workers, servants, craftsmen, traders, industrialists, civil servants, teachers, lawyers, and doctors are emerging. They are well-dressed, well-fed, and well-housed, they will be sitting by the radio and lamp at night and in a seat with a book and newspaper next to them. They will tell their children of their grandfather, who complained that the black race was disappearing because no one believed in the sorcerer anymore.

Johannes, I repeat. Not a single white man is here to bring you civilization; my country is here to make profits. The missionaries bring you Christianity. If they knew for sure that your civilization undermined that belief, they would certainly fight it. The other white men are here, without exception, to earn money. But everything that the missionaries and other white men do, everything that my country does here, brings European civilization to you, and that is of immeasurable value to you.

You can't wish for anything other than that, and, as I have already said, we can't do anything else than be here."

Johannes spoke softly and worthily:

"I thank you, Mr. Beddegenoot. I have understood well, it is the truth. Now I ask you to also understand me. If the white man tells me, 'Dirty *macaque*, here is a thousand francs,' I don't want his money. If he tells me, 'Dirty *macaque*, here is civilization,' then I say, 'Keep your thousand francs, keep your civilization, leave my country so that you can't call me a dirty *macaque* ever again'."

"You are very right," Beddegenoot said, "all civilizations piled up together would not justify that for me."

All felt sudden deep sympathy with the young man who, with cast down eyes, stood motionless and deeply touched in front of them.

"You know," said Father Edward in his Flemish dialect from Turnhout, "this young man keeps bringing up the same thing. They are overly sensitive. A good word means everything to them, and, as soon as they get some education, humiliation becomes real torture for them."

Jac. Bergeyck

From a Congolese Perspective

Jac. Bergeyck (Lommel 1914 – Leuven 1991) is the pseudonym of Jacques Antoon Theuws. From 1947 to 1959, he worked as a Franciscan missionary in Katanga. Besides his activities as a missionary, he completed a doctoral dissertation in anthropology in 1953. In the 1960s and 1970s, he pursued an academic career, working as a professor at the Lovanium University in Leopoldville (today's Kinshasa), the Université Officielle du Congo in Elisabethville (today's Lubumbashi), and Windsor University in Canada. His anthropological research has a direct bearing on his literary work, which consists of poetry, short stories, and novels.

Placied Tempels' famous study *Bantoe-filosofie* (1945; Bantu Philosophy) had a strong influence on Bergeyck. Building on the work of a number of predecessors, Tempels not only made a thorough analysis of the African worldview but also stressed that the Catholic Church had to adapt to African culture. It was a revolutionary proposal, which brought him into conflict with the Catholic authorities in the Congo, who were proponents of a top-down approach to evangelization. Tempels was consequently recalled to Belgium but allowed to return to the Congo after a few years.

In Bergeyck's literary works, African culture and society and the way in which they affect the behavior of the individual take center stage. His novella *Het onzekere hart* (The Uncertain Heart) appeared in 1959. It was followed by *De levende doden* (1960; The Living Dead), *Het levende beeld* (1962; The Living Statue), *Het stigma* (1970; The Stigma), *De pofadders* (1975; The Puffadders), *Een tuin die niet van Eden was* (1985; A Garden Not From Eden), *Het orakel* (1987; The Oracle), and *Verhalen uit Kongo* (1988; Stories from the Congo).

In the collection *Verhalen uit Kongo*, Africans are the main characters. Although references are repeatedly made to the winds of political change sweeping through the Congo, the Africans and African society are presented as largely untouched. Despite the political upheaval, the conversion of many to Catholicism, and the expansion of the school network, the old beliefs and traditions retain a tight grip on the individuals. Witchcraft and the spirits of the ancestors also continue to hold sway. Africans live in a state of constant fear, suspicion, and alertness but are unable to free themselves from the evil forces bedeviling their life. Kapya, the main character of the short story "The Storm," for instance, is weighed down by the curse that appears to rest on his wife, Nyota. Bergeyck's short stories sketch a dark portrait of the lives of the Congolese. They are written with verve and, as a result of his intimate knowledge of African culture, bear the stamp of authenticity. A reader may wonder, though, to what extent this despondent picture of African society and of the lives of Africans corresponds to reality as perceived by the Congolese.

Extract originally published as:
Bergeyck, J. *Het onweer*, in: *Verhalen uit Kongo* (Brecht: De Roerdomp, 1988), 28–36.

Translated with permission from Minderbroeders Vlaanderen.

The Storm

The night is heavy. It pushes constantly on the adobe walls of the hut like a living weight. This makes the darkness inside even more suffocating. The darkness pants between the walls, under the heavy roof of straw and bamboo. There is no window, no chimney, no opening. Just a door, if you could call it that, tightly closed with bamboo wickerwork. Kapya lies naked on his mat but isn't asleep. Black in the darkness, he is invisible. His eyes, opened wide, stare without seeing anything. He is part of the night. The darkness weighs on his face, on his chest, on his hands, on his limbs.

The night is sultry. He has never known a night so black and heavy. He sweats from a stifling anguish. The smell hangs like a biting smoke invisible in the darkness. All things have lost their form. The night has no face. The night is an immeasurable threat. It has no name, no form, no borders. The night holds death and life. No one knows what is born out of this darkness.

Kapya lies lost in the darkness, and fear sits like a barb on his heart. The child awakens convulsively in the mother's womb and grasps blindly for people. The night is like a mother's womb. The night holds the people like the heavily agitated womb of beginning. Each awakening is like being born, painfully rolling over from death to life.

This night and this sultry hut are worse than the mother's womb. The nameless darkness keeps growing, impervious and unrecognizable, into a deadly threat.

Kapya dreams with his eyes open.

Next to him lies his young wife. He doesn't see her but feels her presence intensely. He touches her body and feels assurance and peace in the warm movement of her sides. Her breath is a controlled power which makes the darkness move. The night pants on with the breathing of his wife. She is familiar with the night. She also stores death and life in the night of her womb. His clammy hand slides along her smooth loins. Her sleep is deep and certain, without dreams; it is one with the great movement of the world. Her breathing is in all things. She is present, deep and inseparable, in all darkness, in all becoming, in every gestation.

In what strength is her peace rooted? Nyota…. she smells good in her sleep; she doesn't smell of sweat and fear. Where is her world? Where is her soul? Her secret shadow? Does she possess the secret of life and death? Now she is dark like the night.

Trembling, his desperate hand touches her strong breast. She sighs in her healthy, unmoved sleep. She sleeps in complete abandonment. Her peace, her light breathing, and her coolness restrain the ghosts and chase the darkness to the walls. Kapya sweats from restlessness.

For how many months had she been his wife? Even before the dowry was paid, he claimed his rights. His audacious overconfidence continually consumed this fruitless mystery. Her womb was like the night, full of dismay, barren, infertile. She grew death in it. His power weighed in his own limbs, like the surplus resin that squeezes through the bark of the trees. His wife was like the night, full of secret danger, uncontainable, impermeable. She became his secret fear.

Other women who had accompanied her as brides to the village had already given birth multiple times. There had been shouts of joy. The women had covered themselves with clay and the men had called to God with loud voices, praising the ancestors and glorifying life. His wife remained barren, solid and hard like a statue in shining wood. Her body was slender, muscular like a man, strong and supple like a young palm tree. But nothing bloomed in her. Her quiet comings and goings, her meager words, her soft willingness, her vague smile – everything was a riddle. She became like the forest, impenetrable.

A bird sailed through the night and shouted shrilly: *"Nswee! Nswee! Nswee!"* Kapya was surprised. His wife moved in her sleep. Did she recognize the shout of the witches? This was the shout of the witches who left behind their bodies in the houses by night. Their magic soul, their shadow, became a black bird. They flew invisibly through the sky, robbing the living souls from defenseless people and holding witches' meals in hidden, bleak places. His wife moaned in her sleep. Kapya was lying immobile. He shivered from fear. Once again, he heard the cry of the bird already far away: *"Nswee! Nswee! Nswee!..."*

Then he recalled his years at the missionary school. Together with other young men, he left his village and went to school to learn new things: reading, writing, and arithmetic. He still remembered the things he had learned: the names of rivers, roads, plains and mountains. He set up traps, hunted rats, grasshoppers, fowl, or wild cats. He still partly clung to the old laws and customs. As a child, he had been spoiled, cherished by his mother. He lived, ate and slept at her breast or on her back. But once weaned, he was trained for the rough life of men. He was thin and scraggy, but tough like bamboo. Then he heard of the wonders in the school, and he also wanted to know and own these new things. His head rumbled from strange words, letters and numbers, weights and measures. His imagination became a jungle. There, civilization and history were recreated according to Kapya's own image and likeness: Ulaya! The words about God were less strange to him. His name was as familiar to him as bow and arrow. Here, the word got a new gloss, a new depth … but everything else that was told about Kirisito remained in his thoughts like a vague and strange tale. He had listened to it as he did to the old myths, which were told at night around the fire. Wondrous things that happened a long, long time ago. Only good storytellers could make those things come back to life.

One day, the drums beat their shuddering force through the villages. The young generation had to start a new phase in life and celebrate the transition from childhood to manhood. For several nights in a row, the drums resounded, shrill voices sang, and heavy feet danced. The village stank of beer, sour, and lust. One evening, Kapya was seized and, with ferocious howling, dragged into the wilderness. Before he knew what had happened, he felt a pain like a thousand arrows in his body. He shook and bent like a bow. He almost fainted, bit his lips and ground his teeth. Then it stopped. He became hard as stone, slept naked on the ground in the open air, withstood hunger and cold, ran the gauntlet for alleged mistakes and controlled his rebelliousness. Every abuse, every manly secret sunk in his afflicted heart like a seed. From there his manhood would grow, bound, inalienable, fixed in his possession. From that restrained power he would live, always. His heart would never be empty.

When he came back to the village, dressed in his raffia dance skirt, with his face painted like a warrior, pale and thin, his mother had shouted out of relief and pride: "*Nkambo*! – Father!"

He never saw a school again. He stayed in the village, only travelling to friends and relatives, and learned to live life like a free-born man.

Nyota was the daughter of a *mfumu*, a person of high rank. Her mother was his third wife. As a child, Nyota lived in and around the kitchen of her mother, calm as a girl in a harem. She played silently around the hut, was solitary by nature and had little interaction with the children of the other wives. She followed her mother to the well and to the field, learned the little household tasks while playing and barely heard the quarrels that filled the days.

The day she was no longer a girl, her mother yelled the big news to the neighbors. There was a feast with beer and dance and she resigned herself to undergoing the old rituals and customs to ensure her fertility. The transition to a higher social rank took six months. During six months, she was purified from childhood and formed into a woman. Day by day, she was led deeper into the glimmering world of the women. She listened to their secrets and received the marks of it on her own body. She learned the secrets of their hidden power, the knowledge of darker things: the changing moons and the rolling power of fertility and germinating life, of rain, fire, and heat. She learned of all the wondrous powers which affected and controlled fields, animals and humans.

Now, Nyota was no longer a child. The man who wanted to marry her could come. She didn't fear him; she felt confident thanks to her knowledge. She was healthy in her body and soul; the silliness of her childhood was washed off in the flowing water of the river.

Kapya wanted to have her. He had brought the first gift to the bride. His father had done the rest: talking, drinking, more talking and solemnly sealing the deal. Everything had taken its slow course: gifts and presents, fetching the bride, speeches and rituals and the nightly feast. In the morning the "ashes were swept out of the fireplace." These were the ashes of the single life. The marriage was solemnized.

In her new state, Nyota was the way she was with her mother: willing and solitary. This was the bright beginning. Nyota was strong, used to the heavy work of women, submissive, calm, and assured.

Each time Kapya called her "into the house," because he was still young and restless, her voice was just as flat as when he asked for water: "*Mfumwami* – My lord!" Each time anger made him unreasonable, or he was rude or grumpy, she always gave in: "*Eo! Eo!*"

This unchangeable peace and assurance caused his first doubt. She was not like the other women. Why didn't she complain? Where did she keep her anger hidden?

The day he came home drunk, he had screamed loudly, scolded her for being a slut and an animal. She didn't answer. Anger darkened his mind, but she had evaded his wild blows. She prepared his food and covered him up after he fell asleep.

Kapya was uncertain. Her smile was secretive. He kept an eye on her glance. Wasn't her eye angry? Her womb stayed barren; her hard body remained strange to him. However he wrestled, however his entire being convulsively strove to germinate life, he felt futile, shocked, beaten, and broken.

This is how the dancer is. From the weight of his limbs, from the earth and the night he slowly molds the first lines, the first form of his movement. His soul shakes the walls and his zest for life shoots up out of his limbs, his waist and his loins. The dancer creates, recreates his earthly fate to a certain form and clear figures. He wrestles toward the light.

Thus Kapya was wrestling from the deepest impulses of his being to create life in that barren womb. This became irrecoverable. His power did not have the ability to create a form. His wife became deeper than the night. This was no creation but extermination. This was the deadly secret. Instead of life, did she carry the germs of death? She carried her magic potions around her loins; her body had been marked by the magic symbols of the tribe and family. Were these the means to life? Where then did that bitter uncertainty in Kapya's heart come from? There was a slow but deadly poison in him. The moons came and went. The blank light of the moon was the glimmering of the world of the dead; it upset nature. His wife hid herself in her own small hut, rubbed white soil on her forehead and temples. All of life's juices became agitated. From their turbid mixture, new life came into being. His wife left her secure hut. Her womb was purified but just as dark and closed off. Her secret was as impenetrable as the secret of the death. She lived in a kingdom of dusk. His wife was like a ghost. Her hard body, without bloom or fruit, was but an appearance, something of a delusion. She herself was a ghost. Her proximity became an oppression, a menace like a dream, a poisonous growth in the man's heart.

This night was worse than all the others. The humid heat weighed on everything. It became a living being – present everywhere, visible nowhere. Kapya was restless. He moaned from discomfort. Fear thrashed about in the darkness of his heart. His wife slept, imperturbable. Her sleep was cool and deep. This also was just an appearance. This cool body was the empty husk for a soul, which had gone, roaming through the night like a dark bird, invisible.

"Nyota" – Her breath rustled calmly.

"Nyota!" His trembling hand touched her naked shoulder.

"Nyota!" – She sighed in her sleep.

Then the first thunder rolled loudly through the night. The lightning beast scampered along the clouds.

Kapya cried: "*Mvula!* – rain."

The thunderclaps tumbled like mountains over each other … balls of fire splashed, popping open. His wife threw her arms open. Did she call the lightning? Dismay overtook him. Did she call the fire, death in unspoken curses?

Crackling, the singing fire beat through the roof and walls. Choking, the smell of fire crawled into his throat, his mouth, his eyes. The roof caught fire. The sound in his scorched throat was like a cry of death. Like a wild animal shot by a hunter, he tore the door and the wall to smithereens and ran through the village in a panic.

The rain howled over the plain, plunged into trees and houses, it whipped like a scourge through the night, merciless, foaming, like a primeval destruction.

Then it became light. The earth steamed and the first sunlight was red like blood. Kapya still shuddered from dismay in front of his charred hut. Suddenly he saw Nyota. Like a statue, hard and smooth. Absent and unaware she sat under the awning of a neighboring house. She was barely dressed in a pitiful piece of clothing. Her being, her face, and her vague smile were closed off and enigmatic.

Months of fear and anguish erupted out of Kapya. He cringed, pointed in immeasurable anger to his wife and yelled hoarsely: "*I abe mfwisi*: you are a witch! You called the lightning fire! You sought my death, always, always, with magic, with lightning, with the power of the dead and the living! You…"

Before he could curse her, Nyota had jumped up. She put her arms around her head protectively and, screaming, fled from the destructive anger: "*Yoo! Yoo! Lolo! Lolo!*"

A short time later Kapya walked along the main road, which crossed the interior of the country. He carried his scarce possessions in a bundle on his back. The old men of his clan had already departed for Nyota's village to reclaim the dowry.

Kapya kept walking, staring straight ahead. His heart and head were still full of dark clouds, like the sky after a storm. He went to meet a new world, Kizungu, the city of the white men. There his fear would die. This was a new beginning. This was a flight.

Piet van Aken

Cynical Power Struggles

Piet van Aken (Terhagen 1920 – Antwerp 1984) was a socially committed writer, best-known for the novella *Klinkaart* (1954). In 1959, he published the novella *De nikkers* (The Negroes). The story is based on a strike for a pay raise organized in 1941 by the laborers of a copper mine of the Union Minière mining company near Elisabethville (Lubumbashi). The strikers, who had gathered in the soccer stadium for a protest meeting, were fired upon by the Force Publique, the colonial army. Dozens of people died. Van Aken, who never visited the Congo, studied the file on the strike at the Socialist Workers Union, where he was the editor of the journal *De werker* (The Worker).

De nikkers has the district administrator Robert Meersman as its main character. He provides his version of a strike at the Kazambashi mine in Belleville ("beautiful city"), cynically rebaptized Bedville ("Bed city") by the Belgians. In his account, the events surrounding the strike get more attention than the strike itself. Consequently, the strike becomes almost incidental. The Belgians are mainly concerned with the protection of their privileges, the maintenance of their authority, and the battling out of their mutual disagreements. The shift in focus from the strike to the quarrels among the Belgians is an illustration of colonial policy itself: it too makes the Congolese the victims of Belgian self-interest. The strike is suppressed in blood. Clausen, the provincial governor, and his wife are killed in an ambush. For Meersman, life continues as before.

In this novel, all Belgians are guilty of the misuse of power: the mining company that does not want to give in to the pay demands of the laborers; the missionaries who send the adherents of the Kitawala religion (an African offshoot of the Jehovah Witnesses) to a reeducation camp; and the civil servants who are only concerned about their careers. Meersman finds these forms of misuse of power ineffective and even counterproductive. But he himself is not better than the others. He is a sly manipulator who uses people to further his own personal agenda: survival in a world shaped by the brutal use of power. *De nikkers* presents the colonial set-up as a power struggle in which the powerful pitilessly exploit the powerless. The novella ends with a confirmation of the status quo. At the same time, it suggests that the present situation will not last much longer. A facade of meekness masks absolute disdain. The scene in which Cathérine, the mulatto girl Meersman is in love with, spits on him after he has raped her illustrates a tension that will inevitably erupt in violence.

> **Extract originally published as:**
> Piet van Aken. *De nikkers* (Antwerp: Houtekiet, [1959] 2001), 105–112.

The Negroes

"Edward is dead," I said.

She said: "Ah," and closed her eyes, and I thought that I saw the brown skin of her neck move as if she swallowed. "I heard the shots. And then I saw the vultures."

I said: "It didn't have to happen," and I meant it.

"The Negroes say that it is the fault of the *bulamatari*," she said. "They say that the *bwana* administrator is a righteous man, but that the *bulamatari* called the soldiers to Kazambashi. They say that his soul is blacker than a Negro's skin." Her voice sounded soft and casual, as if she was talking to herself, but, I suspected, as I had not expected to, that there was a concealed meaning behind her words, and I hoped that I was wrong.

"I notified Edward," I said.

"With words," Cathy said. "Words hardly ever help. They don't cause you any pain. They only hurt the foolish. They don't kill you. If you had notified me then that Kasaji was an impending danger for me, I would have probably laughed at you. It was good that you didn't notify me."

"I didn't have the time," I said.

"No."

"Even if I had gotten the time, it would not have helped; there is no possible defense against Kasaji."

She said: "Ah," again, and drew a puff on her cigarette and held the smoke in her lungs as long as she could hold her breath. "I would have laughed at you. Back then I still thought I wasn't a Negro. That was partly your fault, *bwana* Robert. Not because of the look in your eyes; there are other white men who think it's great to sleep with a Negro girl. No, it was because of the way you restrained yourself. As if you had respect for me. As if I wasn't black, but your equal; as if I had only been tanned by the sun."

"This is how it feels for me, too."

"It is very important. If I had already thought differently about myself then, I would have immediately given in to you. I would have been proud that a *bwana* administrator wanted to go to bed with me. Do you realize how important it was?"

I didn't know what to reply and mumbled something between my teeth and didn't even try to understand it myself.

She smiled sourly and shifted with a lazy, nimble movement of the hips and I thought that the bedbugs had probably finally succeeded in making her aware of their presence. "It was hubris. Actually, it was a misunderstanding; because my skin was more brown than black and because I spoke French better than many *bwanas*, I thought that I wasn't a Negro. Even when I had to appear in front of you and receive the stamp for Kasaji, I still refused to believe that I was black. Even when I arrived in Kasaji. And during the first weeks in the camp. Have you ever been to Kasaji, *bwana* administrator?"

I said: "No. It is only a name, and a dot on the map." My voice sounded hoarse and my throat itched.

She said: "From the first day, the camp manager had the same look in his eyes as you do, and that didn't help me clear up the misunderstanding. It was as if I had ended up among a load of blacks by mistake. As if someone had played a trick on me and would be sorry for it and would want to quickly rescue me from the camp. I acted as if I didn't notice the look in the eyes of the camp manager. After a few days he was chasing me and didn't even try to hide what he wanted from me." She was quiet for a while and dropped the half-smoked cigarette next to the bed, and I put my foot on it. For some inexplicable reason, I expected what was going to come next and felt that I could have killed that unknown camp manager with my bare hands. And then she began to speak again. I sat imprisoned in a sort of pleasurable horror about the casual, detached, emotionless tone in her voice and was devoured by a blind fury because she wasn't bitter. "Kasaji is beautiful. There is no other place here that is so beautiful and fertile. I didn't see a lot of it. All I saw was an endless cassava field. Every day we had to weed. Every evening we cut the sand fleas out of our skin with a thorn. We became incredibly skilled at that. Every evening we also received our allotted portions of whipping. I didn't. Not the first weeks. The manager ensured each time that I was nearby whenever the black people received their rations of the *chicote*. He settled his gaze on me. I looked at the back of a Negro who was being beaten; he had to take his pants off and go on his hands and knees and let himself be beaten. They had a ruse, which for a long time was passed down by the old timers to the newbies; while they rested on their elbows, they ensured that they protected their balls with their hands. First, it seemed silly and needlessly ridiculous to me. You saw the skin on their back break open and you saw the Negroes jumping up after each hit as if they stuck to the whip when it was pulled up high for the following blow. You heard them cry like young animals, but they never forgot to keep their balls in their hands. They were afraid of the whip, but their fear only concerned the pain. They knew that they would forget it after a couple of days. What they truly feared was that they would get an unexpected kick in their underbelly. It seemed as if nothing bothered them after a while, as long as their balls were protected. As if they, without exception, wanted to spend the rest of their lives in bed after their release. In the beginning, I found it foolish, but later I understood them."

I said with grim mocking: "You don't have to be a Negro to understand that."

"As long as I could keep the camp manager at bay, I didn't have to fear the black guards. But after a few weeks he got impatient. He used to call me the radio singer and asked me sometimes when I would come sing for him alone. Whenever he wanted to be funny, I could easily handle him; he didn't even speak decent French. But the longer it went on, the less funny he became. After a few weeks, he didn't speak to me anymore. He avoided me, and I thought that he had concluded that it wasn't worth the risk. Two days later I got my share of the *chicote*. The black guard who managed the whip spared me. I barely had any pain.

It was just as if I had burned my back, or as if a burning branch had fallen on my back. I was surprised the other Negroes went berserk as if they had their throat cut when they were beaten. Afterwards, I was able to go to the infirmary by myself. There was a doctor there who ensured that you didn't get infected. The doctor was an old man who was always drunk but who knew his job. He regularly gave us ointments to heal the wounds when we cut out the sand fleas. He patched me up and gave me a room where I would sleep for the night. When I woke up, two guards were holding me, and the manager stood there, grinning at me while he undid the buttons of his pants."

I said angrily: "All you have to do is put that in a report, and I will not rest until that filthy dog is kicked out overseas."

Without changing her tone, she said: "I'm not complaining. All he did was make me understand that I am only a Negro girl. He did nothing with me that he wouldn't have done with the blackest Negro girl. While I was lying there I understood. I didn't even scream and didn't struggle. He was too dumb to even think about that. He thought that it was submissiveness, the old, dumb pliability, the slavishness of the Negroes. He didn't even understand that it was the most groundless form of contempt that I could muster up. He was a tall, coarse brute with red hair. His eyes were brown, ugly, with a type of slimy yellow through the white. All that time I saw those eyes just above me."

I bent down and put my hand roughly on her mouth, pushing as hard as I could. I said: *"Me napenda we sawa sawa samaki napenda maie"* and started to gasp. She looked calmly to me without an attempt to defend herself and it suddenly hit me that I was hurting her. I took my hand away as if I had burned it and when I clenched it into a fist, I felt her spit between my fingers. I repeated: "I love you, Cathy, I love you" and had the silly, irrational hope that my words broke through the time and defused what had happened to her in faraway Kasaji.

She quickly rubbed her lips with her tongue. "All that time I only saw his eyes," she said. "I didn't feel the pain of my wounds anymore, where the whip had opened my back. It seemed to me that I wouldn't ever be able to be harmed anymore. I barely felt how he moved in me. All that time I paid attention to his eyes and when I noticed that he was going to come I spat. He struggled upright and cursed and rubbed his eyes and then he laughed and hit me twice in my face. My one eye was closed. And then he said that he would let the black men have their way with me. He went away and the black men tried it, but they didn't have any fun. A Negro doesn't do it if he isn't having any fun. They soon stopped and left me alone."

I said, hoarse with rage: "Bastard." I stared down at the thin scar and followed it with my eyes from her shoulder to her breast. I lost all track of time and a power outside of myself forced my hand down until my stretched fingers touched her skin. Her breast was warm and plump. I felt the unevenness of the scars and suddenly my hand began to tremble. I stared down at it while the shakiness sizzled up along my arm until my entire body seemed filled with it. I went to sit on the edge of the bed and snatched the blouse out of the skirt, heard the fabric tear and put my hands on her shoulders.

"The one who sent me to Kasaji was a wise man," said Cathy.

"Not for me. For me you are just as Greek as Wilders' wife. Once you return to the radio tomorrow, everything will be just as before. You will forget Kasaji once you are working again."

"I will not forget Kasaji. What I learned there is much too important. After that first night, I learned to do it like the Negroes. I did it first with a *kitawala* preacher; I felt the scars on his back while we were doing it and it was not like with the white brute. I felt him everywhere inside me, and, even long afterwards, it seemed as if I still felt him inside."

I shook her roughly. She just let it happen and her head fell limp on the bed when I let her go. "You're talking nonsense," I said fiercely.

"I got pregnant, and an old *kitawala* cooked herbs for me. I was sick the whole night and thought that I was going to die. The supervisor came into the shack and I saw his face while he stood inspecting me. My only thought was that I would be safe from him for a while now. The doctor tended to me and ensured that I would be left in peace. But I didn't want to be left in peace anymore. When I came here, I had a desire to do it with Edward Malela, but his wife made a fuss and Edward himself cared only about the Kazambashi."

I hit her in the face; not hard, but powerfully enough, the way you would hit an epilepsy patient who was getting an attack. "You're talking nonsense," I repeated.

She answered softly, with a strange complaining undertone in her voice: "No. It was important. Sometimes I thought about the man who had sent me to Kasaji and I imagined that his face was bent over me. Sometimes I thought of you and regretted that I hadn't given in to your desire at that time. I tried to understand what had driven my mother towards that Negro. I had the impression that I would track it down whenever I repeated it with you in reverse. And sometimes I thought that you were the man who sent me to Kasaji, *bwana* Robert."

She barely got the time to say the last words aloud. My hand popped out and clamped her neck in the circle formed by finger and thumb and pinned her to the mattress. Even then she didn't fend for herself. She looked up at me and her eyes seemed to get gradually larger and darker until it seemed that I was surrounded entirely by their sad radiance. I could have choked her without any effort. And then she whispered "ah," and moved her hips hardly noticeably, and I said hoarsely: "Cathy," and kept whispering her name while I let myself fall over her. Afterwards it was just like I had tried to imagine countless times whenever I came home heated and drunk after a fruitless visit to her flat. It did not bother me that I didn't smell her body but the bad stink of Ptoia. It did not bother me either that I thought about what had happened to her at Kasaji. Or that I knew that I had spoken the truth when I told her that I loved her the way a fish loves the water. And that I would be pushed to her again and again after this night. When I lifted myself up again, panting, she spat strongly in my face.

Jan van den Weghe

A Plea for Cooperation

Jan van den Weghe (Halle 1920 – Attenhove 1988) was a poet, novelist, and essayist. From 1952 to 1960, he held different positions in the colonial Department of Education in the Congo and in Burundi, a former German colony that came under Belgian control after World War I.

The short story "De inlandse schoolmeester" (The Indigenous Schoolteacher) appeared in the collection *Kinderen van Kongo* (1965; Children of the Congo). It is set in 1958. A black teacher, Pierre Maledego, gets drawn into a conspiracy against the Belgians. The conspirators want to drive the colonials out of the Congo because they believe that Belgium has brought the Congolese nothing but misery. For a while, Maledego plays along with the conspirators before turning against them.

The ideological core of the short story is the speech given in 1958 by a Belgian head teacher to the teaching staff of his school on the fiftieth anniversary of the annexation of the Congo by Belgium. In his address, the principal gives his view on the future of the Congo, proclaiming that Belgians and Congolese should work closely together to safeguard what has been achieved. In his view, the colonizers can justifiably claim certain rights to the Congo through their civilizing efforts. Moreover, he asserts, most Congolese are still living like the Europeans did two thousand years ago. As a result of these different levels in civilization, the Africans need the Belgians.

The author illustrates the Congolese's lack of civilization by denying them all rationality and morality, presenting them as naive, manipulative, cruel, superstitious, primitive, power hungry, and licentious. Even though he is an *évolué*, Pierre Maledego is tarred with the same brush and described as an incompetent, lazy teacher. Moreover, Maledego himself thinks in similar terms of the other *évolués*. The portrait he sketches of them is dismally negative. In contrast to the Congolese, the head teacher, the only Belgian character appearing in the short story, has exclusively positive character traits. He has empathy for the Congolese, tries to help them as best he can, and fervently believes in collaboration between the races. "De inlandse schoolmeester" suggests that the Congolese cannot cope with the freedom independence brings. Consequently, the Europeans will be needed for a long time to guarantee a prosperous future for the Congo.

Van den Weghe reiterates the traditional colonial stereotypes: the Europeans are inspired by the ideal of bringing civilization to the Congolese, but the Congolese are the ungrateful recipients of their civilizing efforts. While it is the intention of the author to demonstrate the childishness of the Africans who will have to remain under the paternalistic supervision of the whites for the near future, his blatantly manipulative interventions only demonstrate his own prejudices. Maledego, who makes an utter fool of himself and his fellow blacks, is all too clearly a puppet manipulated by the author. "De inlandse schoolmeester" makes it clear how widespread and rooted the European superiority complex still was in the 1960s and how firmly ingrained the paternalistic attitude of the author, and, by extension, of many other Belgians toward the Congolese.

> **Extract originally published as:**
> Van den Weghe, J. *De inlandse schoolmeester* (1965), in: *Kinderen van Kongo* (Brussels: Manteau, 1965), 33–40.
> Translated with permission from Standaard Uitgeverij.

The Indigenous Schoolteacher

The white man does not speak in a sentimental way. He speaks well. Sometimes, a little pensively, he looks at us and says, "Since the situation has changed, what measures must we take now? What does the future of the Congo look like? It may seem unbelievable, yet we are only at the very start of solving this problem. But the Belgians are practical people. They don't like poking the bear, they claim. However, it now seems as if the bear has been provoked. So some adjustments are urgently required. It's not without reason that the title 'Ministry of Colonies' has been changed to 'Ministry of the Belgian Congo and Ruanda-Urundi.' That could be very important, but it is also entirely possible that it means nothing. The fact that the authorities deemed it necessary to implement this name change is, however, symptomatic. For the white people, the moment has come in which they are confronted with the question: Are we only here for a little bit longer, or are we building a definitive political home here, of which we will be the co-builders and co-owners? The Congolese population will at one time come to full political maturity. One must wish that this will happen quickly. It is simply unthinkable that Congo will continue to be governed from Brussels for a long time. It also doesn't seem possible that the Congolese population will send representatives to the Belgian parliament because there they would immediately form the absolute majority. Will we become a federal state, a dominion, a confederacy? Considering the way things are right now, I must say that it is too early to answer this question directly. And I would want to add that it is maybe already too late…"

"You're right…," Damange whispers.

I nod and the white man continues: "Meanwhile a quick evolution is urgently needed. On this, many agree in principle, but the question remains: How should we tackle it? It is a problem that must be solved at the highest level, but very unfortunately, I have the impression that we are not fully aware of the problem at the highest level and don't seem particularly concerned about it… I fear that we will have to face serious consequences if blind reactions aren't to be curbed by the appropriate means. There is a time for everything, but, if one lets the moment pass, it is too late. I honestly believe that the hourglass is almost full. But I also honestly believe that this country can still be saved, if we all understand one another well and want to work together. The Congo will not be saved by troublemakers and instigators. Our salvation lies in mutual comprehension and mutual understanding. Let me ask you: Is it abuse whenever we, white people, whom many of you already hate, speak of our intention to definitively settle in this country? Is that unjust to the native population? In all honesty: I would answer this question negatively. We whites, are, I believe, not unjust, when we say that we want to stay here. And why not? For many reasons, which I won't elaborate on here. But I do want to draw your attention to an important aspect of the matter with a simple question: What was the Congo before the arrival of the Europeans? I know that this is not a pleasant question, but one must dare to face the truth. Well? What was the Congo some decades ago? It was a place where tribes and clans lived persistently in mutual enmity, poor, in primitive huts, without hygiene. They were threatened by illness, hunger and ruthless slave drivers, who found willing allies in some chiefs, eager for booty. These are facts, historical facts!"

Damange nudges me with his elbow again. "He is lying," he whispers. "Benjamin Franklin said: History teaches us that we can't learn anything from history." I nod and keep listening to the white man. "What was the situation here in Katanga?" he asks. "It used to be a large wasteland before. The Europeans discovered rich copper ore here. Hardly any natives lived here. The current inhabitants were largely brought here by the Europeans. They also brought life and welfare here. No one can deny that at least. I will not claim that they did this only for the native people. I know better. But they did it. This isn't about moral service, but about facts, and facts are more honorable than the Lord Mayor of London, as you know. Did the Europeans not acquire a certain right here then? I believe that they possess a sacred right here, namely the right to work. And not only a right, but also a holy duty to bring the task, which they started, to a good end. By their work, the Europeans created the Congo out of nothing – administratively, economically, and politically. The Congo simply wouldn't exist without them. At that time, there was no powerful state here. There was no nation. There was no civilization. The natives didn't know anything of administration, economics, political organizations, or reading and writing. They didn't even know the wheel and the lever. These words may sound harsh, but you all know that they're true. You also know that many Europeans mean very well regarding you. You know that you can put your trust in a lot of us. The bad white people will disappear. They placed themselves outside the community and the new community will simply force them out. But can one actually build a Belgian-Congolese nation? One talks a lot about it. One writes about it. But is it actually possible? Burdeau said once: A nation is a shared dream of the future. A nation is thus a community of people who are prepared to live together and fight through thick and thin. They share a patrimony, based on a culture, on norms and economic interests. They want this patrimony to bloom and, with this goal in mind, make an effort together. The differences in skin color don't matter in all of this."

"Hear him gabble," Damange chuckles. Again I nod, but now I listen full of zeal. What the white man says is nice.

"The Congolese people possess a collection of spiritual values. These must not be stifled. On the contrary! They must be stimulated and further developed. Belgium and the Congo could be considered two complementary states. The Congo supplies raw materials to Belgian industry. Belgium sends teachers and specialists, without whom it is simply not possible to develop specialized techniques. Pan-Africanism, which is mentioned so often, only relies on geographic details, but the economic and social plans of this movement are utopian. It will still be a while before Africa itself will be able to educate specialists in the areas of research and discovery. That time will come for sure, and the earlier it comes, the better. But in the meantime, it is not enough to continue to educate new generations of intellectuals. In the modern economic world, more is needed than learning information from books by heart. One must be able to find new theories and new applications. I believe that the future of the Congo will be much better safeguarded in the framework of a Belgian-Congolese nation than in that of a problematic Pan-African solution. You know us. You are in many ways closer to us than to some African peoples, who are out to exploit you and retain the benefits themselves. That you can ask for firm guarantees speaks for itself. You have to know that, in the future, you will be provided with everything a civilized person can rightly claim. Precisely for this reason, appropriate forms of transition must be found out of which a true democracy can grow. If those appropriate transitional forms can't be found, this nation could end up in ruins. In the Amazon forest, there are, at this moment, wild Indian tribes who still haven't left the Stone Age.

Do you honestly believe that it is in their interest to cut themselves off from Brazil? You don't think that, do you? When the Western states penetrated the then dark Africa with difficulty, Tsarist Russia overran the vast lands of Siberia, which was and still is populated by a large number of different tribes. Are these all politically autonomous now? I know very well, and consider it only natural that the natives in the Congo hanker for a status that provides equality and respect. It is very gratifying that they have this ambition. It is their obligation and even their holy right. But this equality must obviously be combined with equal responsibility. Equal rights, but also equal obligations. There will come a day when all the natives of the Congo will go to the polling booth. If the omens don't deceive us, that day will come soon. But we should not forget that political democracy must always be preceded by social democracy. And a certain time for learning is required. It is in no way sufficient to prepare only some leaders for that task. They would quickly become tyrants and enslave and exploit their own people. No. We must educate the masses. These masses must choose their own leaders. They must perform checks on the policy of their new leaders. Today this is unfortunately not yet possible. The democratic form of government is without doubt the best and greatest, but it is also by far the most difficult to achieve. Technical progress isn't sufficient to make an entire people mature in no time; a people isn't able to govern itself in a very short amount of time. History teaches us that, and I hope that we won't make big mistakes for the umpteenth time. The goal which you all hanker for can only be the result of education, and the educational process is a slow process. Education in families. Education in schools. Difficult education and, if necessary, remedial education for adults. You only have to look around. Houses are built everywhere. Beautiful, modern schools are being erected everywhere. There is higher education in this country. There are trade unions. Two universities have been established. Progress is being made. But all of this needs to move even faster, since we have to reckon with the understandable but dangerous impatience of countless frustrated people. You, gentlemen, have a special role to fulfill in all this. It isn't enough that you, as educators, complete your task promptly in this school. Even outside of school, you must be educators – educators of your own people. Much depends on you. You must never feel elevated above your less fortunate brothers. You are more advanced than many of your fellow Congolese, but there should be no gap between you and the people. You must remain one of them. That is your obligation. Now more than ever, because we can expect that before long adventurers and table jumpers will revolt, and, if you give them a free pass, they will turn this beautiful country into chaos. I am thinking here of the words one of your brothers wrote: We put our hope in the schools, which every year increase in number all over the Congo. Thanks to these schools, the black people will triumph over ignorance. It was Jean-Francois Iyeky who wrote these wise words. Schools are indeed your strongest weapon. Now it is important to work, to study, to educate the children, and the generations of tomorrow. It is a great task, gentlemen, a formidable task, and an ungrateful task, perhaps. But a task on which the salvation of your country depends. Only in this way will the Congo one day become a modern, happy, prosperous country, where white and black, black and white, stand on an equal footing and will live in good understanding with one another."

For a moment, everything is quiet. The white man wipes the sweat from his forehead. He smiles. I am elated. I have a great desire to clap. This man has a message that is different from that of Saani and Tomoko. They hate the white people. All white people. They only speak of murder and destruction. This man wants to build. He may have a white skin and will never be one of us, but he is a man after my own heart. It is so unfortunate that not all white people are like this man here. Things would be so much better in the Congo. I look around me. It is still very quiet. They all sit a little uncomfortably on the low benches in my classroom and remain silent.

Robrecht De Sadeleer

The Disillusionment of the Colonial

Robrecht De Sadeleer is the pseudonym of Jan Hintjens (Ostend 1928), an agronomist. From 1951 to 1960, he lived in the Tshuapa district of the province of the Equator, first working in the service of the colonial administration and later becoming an independent plantation owner. After receiving threats on his life, he returned with his family to Belgium shortly after the Congo's independence. He was a regular contributor to the periodicals *Band* and *Zuiderkruis* (Southern Cross). The periodical *Zuiderkruis* was established in 1955, with the aim of providing a publication outlet for Flemish literature on the Congo. De Sadeleer's novella *Dorp op Likado* (Village on Likado) appeared in *Band* in 1957. Three years later his novel *Palaver om de ebbe* (1960; Discussion around Ebbtide) was published. In both texts the end of the colonial era is discussed.

Palaver om de ebbe is the only novel dealing with the upcoming independence of the Congo. At the end of the text, the author mentions "Ikela, February 1960." The book has an autobiographical basis. For Jan De Sadeleer, the announcement of the date on which independence will be granted and the subsequent breaking out of riots signify that his task is finished. He is of the opinion that, overall, the colonizers have done an excellent job and that most of them have taken the well-being of the Congolese to heart. De Sadeleer considers the Congo to be his country. When he sees mistrust and hatred in the eyes of Africans, he is completely taken aback. He ascribes this hatred to the fact that the Africans and the Belgians have not come to an understanding of one another, mainly because the latter have not ventured outside their white cocoon. In the end, he feels betrayed and abandoned by both Belgium and the Congo.

The author describes the tragedy of the colonial, who suddenly sees his life's work undone and faces an uncertain future. He is aware of his vulnerable position but cannot stop the course of history. It is obvious to him that independence comes too early and that the Congo is not ready for it. De Sadeleer's defense of the colonial past shows how colonizers like him kept on believing, until the very end of the colonial period, in the colonial ethos and remained convinced of the beneficial nature of their presence in the Congo.

Extract originally published as:
De Sadeleer, R. *Palaver om de ebbe* (Antwerp: Boekengilde Die Poorte, 1960), 112–14.

Discussion around Ebbtide

It is quiet outside.

The heat streams like an overflowing barrel of oil between the plants. It rises into the atmosphere and carries a secret in itself like the development of a pregnancy. Up and down against the poles of the *barza*, ants are running, small black dots that do not know the need to rest even for a second. In that heat, like fluffy pillows, only the insects appear still alive.

We think of the Congo.

We see the events of the last months pass by in our memory like a movie played in fast-forward, like a performance for which there isn't enough time to show the whole thing.

We think of the charred huts, the murdered children, and the people who were killed only because they belonged to a particular clan.

We see the long lines of refugees before our eyes, the abandoned villages, the suffering, and endless cries of woe fall on our country like a downpour of curses.

No, we colonizers didn't want any of this. But this branded us, this is a wound in our heart that may never heal.

Because we loved our Congo wholeheartedly. We loved each other like lovers who long for each other because of our differences, because of all we went through and because of the pain we caused each other.

Now we think with certainty that that lover has betrayed us, that she shows us her claws and says: "We have never loved each other." Now we stand here like the injured lover and are powerless because of our love.

The worst is that we now indeed think that everything between us is irrevocably finished and over.

We feel the distance between us grow day by day and we don't dare to take a step to prevent it. Maybe our enthusiasm has already abandoned us. Maybe we don't find the courage anymore to return. Or maybe we unwittingly have already convinced ourselves of the end.

The end.

We feel it coming toward us like a monster. Intuitively, we have already solved the puzzle and imagined a future based on the years that we passed here. We are each convinced that it is over, that we will carry our nostalgia with us and will long for the pains and the nights in the camp bed, for the lovers and the fevers.

We have always felt like exiles, people expelled from humanity in order to serve humanity.

We've always felt at one with Henry Morton Stanley and with the black slave in chains. We have made their traces a little deeper and have pledged our allegiance to things we never fully understood, let alone managed. But until our last days we will feel connected to the continent that can move people to enthusiasm, that can destroy them or glorify them. But we will throw a stone at no one, not even at those who didn't work, battle, or love here. We can only blame time, the time when Christ on Palm Sunday dragged his cross to Golgotha, from a *gloria* to a *requiem*. We weren't taking into account the time, we who had thought that the sun at the equator delineated the same path each day, and never imagined that it would burn and scorch.

I lay my white hand in that of my black brother and know that in both our eyes the same story will be kept a secret. We've both heard this story; other people will not understand. But therefore it will also stay ours, will always be our own, beautiful story.

After every flood comes an ebb. The worst is that we fear that this time, there will be no more flood, that here everything will wither and flow away.

The worst is that we lack the courage to put up a dam to save us. We have, by this ebb, become disenchanted and convinced that it is too late, that no fresh concrete can stop the catastrophe.

I get up again because the silence between us becomes too painful and I reach for the bottle of beer and fill the three glasses again.

On the *barza*, a wagtail peeps, and goes off in the direction of a red butterfly. It tries to catch the butterfly and then flies away angrily when it sees that the prey, after escaping, sits on my hat on the coat rack, beating its wings.

Daisy Ver Boven

Friendship between Black and White

Daisy Ver Boven (Aarschot 1925) lived in the Congo from 1948 to 1961, first in Oshwe and then in Lower Congo. After independence, she moved to Ruanda-Urundi returning with her family to Belgium in 1961. Her first novel, *La piste étroite* (1960; The Narrow Road), appeared in French and was republished in 2017. *La piste étroite* is a song of praise to the love between Ingrid and Jacques, two young idealistic colonials. The narrative glorifies the colonial ethos by constructing an image of the Belgian colonizers as people deeply committed to the well-being of the Congolese. All her other literary publications are in Dutch, among which the Congo novels *Mayana* (1974) and *Gevierendeeld* (1980; Quartered) and the travelogue *Mpasi ... Weerzien met Kongo drie jaar na de onafhankelijkheid* (1964; Mpasi ... Return to the Congo Three Years after Independence).

Between July 1960 and January 1961, Ver Boven wrote *De rode aarde die aan onze harten kleeft* (1962; The Red Earth Which Clings to Our Hearts). The novel begins in November 1958 and ends shortly after the breaking out of riots following the independence festivities. The main characters are Karin Vandam, a social assistant who works at the Social Center in an African neighborhood of Leopoldville (Kinshasa), and Albert Nsimangi, an *évolué* who is a clerk in the personnel department of the Government-General. His wife Anne works as a supervisor at Karin's Social Center. They are a model évolué family and live according to European standards.

Karin is brimming with idealism and optimism. Her idealism is based on her conviction that the Belgians have done an excellent job in bringing civilization to the Congo. She and her friends are examples of the altruistic mindset of the colonizers. They only have the well-being of the Congolese at heart. For his part, Nsimangi feels crushed between European and African culture. He wonders whether the two cultures can be reconciled and hopes to find a synthesis between Europe and Africa. His hope is shattered with the outbreak of the riots. Karin wants to return to Belgium. In the extract included in the anthology, Nsimangi persuades her that she should first assist the Belgian refugees who are airlifted back to Belgium after having witnessed or suffered terrible atrocities. In the end, Karin also leaves for Belgium while nursing the hope that the Belgians will one day be called upon to return to the Congo.

De rode aarde die aan onze harten kleeft revisits the contrast between "civilization" and "primitive society," which has characterized Belgian colonial literature from its inception. Yet, while Flemish Congo literature trumpeted the victory of the forces of civilization over primitive societies during the colonial period, the tables are now turned on the civilizers. The novel suggests that, after independence, the primitive forces regained the upper hand and that the Congolese reverted to their primitive and barbaric lifestyles and went on a rampage against the representatives of Western civilization. What the Belgians have built is razed to the ground. Despite their best efforts, the colonizers have not succeeded in suppressing the primitive instincts of the Congolese. The peaceful and well-meaning Belgians are no match for the irrational behavior and the violent rage of the Congolese. The novel concludes that the gap between the civilized Western world and the primitive African is simply too large to be bridged. The blame for the violent upheaval which breaks out after independence is squarely put on the Congolese, whose primitive instincts the Belgian civilizers have not succeeded in eradicating.

> **Extract originally published as:**
> Ver Boven, D. *De rode aarde die aan onze harten kleeft* (Brussels: Reinaert, 1962), 249–54.

The Red Earth Which Clings to Our Hearts

"Spend your holidays in Switzerland!" the first neon advertisement said, and pink laughing ladies showed well-to-do gentlemen the shining white mountains against a bright blue sky.

"*Sole mio*, the best blanket!" proclaimed the second neon advertisement, with two lively children jumping hand in hand on a cozy bed with pink sheets and a down blanket.

From the Red Cross stand, where Karin was handing out sandwiches, coffee and fruit, her gaze wandered to the two billboards that still functioned remarkably well. She then looked down on the ragged passengers who wanted to go – not to Switzerland – but home, and whose children had not seen a bed in days…

In only a few days' time, the shiny, modern airport, the pride of the people of Leopoldville, had been transformed into a pigsty. The human suffering that had passed through there somehow still remained, mulling about in the great hall, in the hallways and stairs, against the ceilings with holes and the chandeliers shot to pieces during firefights.

An unbroken river of refugees pushed inside, always new faces, who still looked the same…

Neglected, dead-tired mothers with pale, weeping children. Missionary nuns with dirty, stained clothing and rigid gazes. Silent priests without any luggage, some of them so old that they probably had never imagined that they would have to undertake the journey back home…

Young men with bewildered expressions and hastily bound wounds that had left bloodstains on the shorts and khaki shirts which they were wearing when they were attacked.

Old men with unshaved faces and bags under their eyes, deadly ashamed because they were driven out in this manner and because they hadn't been able to protect their wives and children against the terrible insults and wrongdoings…

Women who had been raped, still with the marks of a fierce but unequal struggle all over their bodies, passively let themselves be taken to the doctor, waited their turn in a line like soldiers to receive some care…

Women on stretchers, who couldn't walk anymore after what they had experienced, were placed along the wall, and a merciful hand pulled the grey blankets high up to their pallid faces…

Women who were supported by spouses and friends and with great care were laid down on mattresses spread on the ground…

Women who were completely stressed out and suddenly, for no reason, began to scream terribly and kick as if they were being assaulted and abused again…

Young girls, children still, who had not been spared by the soldiers and who looked into the world out of rigidly empty eyes, still full of the horror that had no name. Friendly people, inspired with the best intentions, had stuffed their arms with toys and dolls they had found God knows where, but it all came too late, much too late. They weren't children anymore and would never be children again.

Karin buttered the slices of bread and made coffee. That was her task. Day and night, dirty hands kept stretching out to her. Dirty, hungry people greedily attacked the bread and hot coffee, which they heartily slurped like a foretaste of being safe again, home again!

Nsimangi made the sandwiches and arranged them on plates, which he handed over to Karin. They didn't really speak to each other, except when absolutely necessary. Nsimangi avoided looking at Karin; he stood like a dark shadow behind her and worked without pause, without granting himself a moment of rest, as if in penance.

There were only a few Africans left in the airport, practically no workers or technical personnel. Only members of the Red Cross walked to and fro, unloading the airplanes, which supplied food, blankets and medicine. They also carried, like Nsimangi, a Red Cross band around their arm and instinctively tried to behave as unremarkably as possible. They did this because, however apathetic the human flock that moved through the airport appeared, the atmosphere was electrically charged; a spark was enough to cause a disaster.

The refugees didn't speak much either. What they had experienced could not be discussed. Only short words, faltering sentences escaped from their chock-full minds: "Kimpese," they said, "it was such a beautiful mission…" "Inkisi!" "Madimba … we should have known! Why did we stay?"

Lubuta! Kenge! Banningville … like the stations of the Cross, names were recited of places far apart, where the same rampant madness had reigned: Luebo, Gemena … and Boende, Boende!

And still other names, many of which Karen had never heard before, humble little posts, spread across the endlessness of the Congolese interior…

They limped on wounded feet and said: "Barbed wire… They had me walk over barbed wire…"

They said: "Pardon? I cannot hear any more … speak louder! They took out my hearing aid…"

They carried their arms in a sling and said: "Luckily only my arm was broken, imagine if they would have hit me with the butt of their gun on my head!"

They said: "Please give me a sandwich with jam ... no, no meat. They beat out three of my teeth, I have difficulty chewing."

They groped helplessly next to the sandwich offered to them and said: "Without glasses I am not a person! You wonder what they will do with all those glasses they ripped from our faces!"

They asked for no sympathy, no consolation. They offered no friendly gesture to Karin nor any word of thanks. She was one of the mileposts placed by human solidarity on their way of suffering. Fate decided that she was better off than most; she was the one who could still give while they could only receive ... and an unconscious resentment developed among the masses against her, standing alone and untouched on the other side of the table.

Nsimangi remained in the background. He worked silently and without looking up. Two or three other Red Cross volunteers, all white, stood with Karin on the barricades and distributed food.

At a certain moment, late in the evening, two of them were so tired that they lay down on the mattresses placed on the upper level. Karin couldn't do it alone and looked back at her friend.

"Do you want to hand out coffee, Albert?" He nodded, filled the cups with care, so much sugar, so much milk...

"Please, ma'am, coffee!" said the lady who had stood in line, dreaming. When she suddenly saw Nsimangi's black arm in front of her, a hysterical shiver ran over her body.

"I won't take any coffee from you, dirty Negro!" she said fiercely, roughly pushing the cup away.

The hot coffee burned Nsimangi's fingers before his shaking hand could put the cup back on the table. He went to the furthest corner of the Red Cross station and started cutting and buttering new slices of bread with automatic gestures. But the agitated woman followed him with her reproaches.

"Now they're proud that they may offer us a slice of bread here, now that they have taken everything from us! I know for sure that this monkey is only here to enjoy watching our misery!"

Her shrill voice cracked and a restless vibration ran through the crowd, who forgot to stick out their hands for the coffee Karin was offering.

"They're all the same indeed, all sadists! Who knows whether he has also raped women? With his nice face and seductive manners, he is just the type to molest our young women…"

The listeners began to move, and the crowd pushed against the dividing line separating them from the Red Cross station, so they could take a closer look at Nsimangi. The looks became threatening.

"The masses," Karin thought bitterly, "the masses, whether black or white, are no more than a horde of wild animals lusting for prey."

She looked around anxiously, cast an imploring look at Nsimangi, who fortunately saw it and immediately understood. He put the plate with sandwiches in the fridge and walked outside without even one glance at the murmuring crowd. Karin's hint, however, didn't escape the young woman who was close to a nervous breakdown.

"That's how you must treat them!" she said sharply to Karin. "You must indulge them and play along with it! You will see what will come of that! It is that gullibility, that humanity, which has brought us to where we are now! Ridiculous, miserable people we have been! The whip! That is the only language they understand!"

Now that Nsimangi had disappeared, the passion quickly dissipated. Everyone bit eagerly into their sandwich and drank with satisfaction the coffee they had first refused. It gradually grew calmer around the post.

"All passengers with pink tickets to the Boeing," a voice said through the loudspeaker. "All passengers with green tickets to the DC 6." All complicated formalities of normal flights had been reduced to this simple announcement…

Karin could finally take a break. She hung her apron on a hook and went outside to look for Nsimangi. He sat in his favorite position, arms around his knees, on the highest step of the terrace. From there he could see the entire airport and the bustle that prevailed there. Karin sat next to him without saying a word. He turned his head toward her and smiled absently.

"That woman was in hysterics," she said unasked. "Who knows what she has experienced…"

He nodded:

"I know…"

He didn't add a word of hate or reproach, but Karin knew how deep such an insult corroded the soul of a black man. Nevertheless, she was thankful to him for the discretion that he showed in front of her fellow citizens who had suffered so much.

For a while, they looked out over the swirling crowds at the airport – such activity had never occurred in Ndjili. Airplanes landed and others took off every few minutes. Planes of all types of models and all types of nationalities stood close to each other while they were being fueled. An unpleasant smell of oil and burning spread over the chill night air.

The Boeing took off with an ear-deafening roar, and the hot air of the engines covered them with heat. Observers watched with fascination how the fantastic plane slowly and majestically climbed up in the air.

"You should also leave one of these days, Karin," Nsimangi said suddenly.

"Why do you say that, Albert?"

"Because it is time … the last whites are going away. What would you still do here?"

She slowly turned to him.

"I came here for the Africans, Albert."

He laughed deeply in his throat and it sounded like a sob.

"They don't want you anymore, Karin, you must have realized that by now!"

She sat motionless from this slap in the face.

"None of them, Albert?"

"I don't know," he said. "I don't know. I have always thought that I knew a lot and could foresee a lot, but now I don't know anything anymore. I don't know where this is going … our independence was possible on the condition that all white people kept bearing their responsibility. Now that we've chased them all out … now we're headed for chaos, there is no solution left, no solution…"

"Yet," Karin said comforting, "sooner or later a reflection must come, and common sense always triumphs in the long run."

"Not here! Not with us! Now that the blind passion has been awakened, now that disorder reigns, now that no discipline, no honor, no humanity exists anymore … you don't know what more we are capable of…"

Karin rocked restlessly back and forth. Nsimangi's words made her heart as heavy as lead.

"The white people don't need to be afraid that all these crimes will remain unpunished," he said reflectively. "Every European woman will be avenged ten times over. This was nothing in comparison to what will come when the Congolese start fighting amongst themselves … and that's going to come! Very soon."

"No, Albert!"

Karin fought against the despair his words stirred in her. This exodus, this pain, and this misery had to be the end of a disaster – the end and not the beginning of a new one. But she knew that Nsimangi was right, that the people of the Congo were moving towards a very dark time.

"Albert…" she said, and she spoke softly, emphasizing every word as if she was scared that he wouldn't understand her well. "Albert, you said: 'the Congolese don't want you any more' … did you also mean that they don't 'need' me anymore?"

"O Karin!" She saw his white teeth shining in the unbelievably joyful smile that reappeared for the first time on his face again: "How can you even ask such a thing?"

(July 1960 – January 1961)

Jef Geeraerts

Paradise Lost

Jef Geeraerts (Antwerp 1930 – Ghent 2015) was the assistant regional supervisor in Bumba, in the Equator province, from 1954 to 1960. After his return to Belgium with his wife and children, he embarked on a literary career. His breakthrough came in 1969, when his novel *Gangreen 1. Black Venus* – the first novel of the *Gangreen* quartet – was awarded the triennial state prize for prose in Belgium. It was a controversial decision. Piet van Aken, a member of the jury, resigned in protest. The provocative novel shook conservative Flemish society to its core — not because of its racist depictions of black women but because of its anti-Catholic attitude and unrestrained celebration of sexual pleasure.

The novel made Geeraerts into an instant celebrity in progressive circles and propelled him into the position of the foremost writer on the Congo, the subject matter with which he is most closely associated. His first short story "De taaie" (1962; The Tough One) was set in the Congo. The novels *Ik ben maar een neger* (1962; I'm Only a Negro), *Het verhaal van Matsombo* (1966; The Story of Matsombo), *Gangreen 1. Black Venus* (1968), *Gangreen 2. De goede moordenaar* (1972; Gangreen 2. The Good Murderer), and *Goud* (1995; Gold) are also set in the former Belgian colony. After his Congo period, Geeraerts reinvented himself as a writer of thrillers. *De zaak Alzheimer* (1985; The Alzheimer Case), which was made into a movie, was his biggest commercial success.

While Geeraerts made use of autobiographical material in his Congo books, it is obvious that he also turned the facts of his life into fiction. He is the creator of a myth in which he depicts himself as a man in search of his natural self. He revolts against bourgeois society and conservative norms that keep the individual in the straitjacket of propriety and hypocrisy. He turns his back on Western society to embrace exultantly a state of unrestrained natural existence, which corresponds with his innermost yearning. Wild sex and hunting allow him to eliminate all rational thought processes and reach a nirvana of sensual life and instinctive lusts. For Geeraerts, the Congo is a primitive paradise where he can reach the apogee of a natural life. Obviously, his white Catholic wife is an obstacle on his road to self-discovery and fulfillment. He disdains and rejects her as a representative of a hated unnaturalness and Western rigidity.

The novel *Schroot* (Scrap) was published in 1963. Its main character, Harry, is an old colonial who was forced to leave the Congo after it gained its independence. His memories swirl around Mbamba and Julie, with whom he had a passionate and harmonious relationship. Half a year after his repatriation to Belgium, he returns to the Congo as a technical adviser. Julie's affair with the Swedish head of the humanitarian UN Mission means the end of their relationship. Harry returns to Belgium, where he cannot adapt to the people and the country. He feels like scrap. In a pub, Harry meets Bob, another colonial repatriate, who fiercely criticizes the colonization of the Congo.

> **Extract originally published as:**
> Geeraerts, J. *Schroot* (1963), 2nd ed. (Antwerp: Manteau, 1990), 202–07. Translated with permission from Standaard Uitgeverij.

Scrap

"Do you know what slowly ruins us, the colonizers, here in Belgium?"

"No," Harry said, "I don't know." He sits curled up in his leather jacket and looks over Bob's head towards the opposite wall with the big-breasted Coca-Cola girl.

"It is difficult to put my finger on it. It is something like ... selling valuable material as scrap." He waits a little, looks Harry right in the eyes. His fox-like face is tense. "In the Congo, we all bore responsibility," he says agitatedly, "we could take the initiative. Our work was good work, great work. It was worth the effort. We had a mission, an ideal. That is what it was. It could satisfy you. And you could breathe. You lived. You lived in a great young country where you could breathe. But now..." he made a helpless gesture.

"Director Ndekemopele, the great idealist," said Harry mockingly, "Oh yes, especially at the end you could really talk of a mission, an ideal. You can't believe how that satisfied me. Sometimes I could scream out of satisfaction."

"And the Belgian government who treated us like dogs. I still remember how De Schrijver said on the radio: 'The officials who cannot continue their careers in normal circumstances can leave their posts. They will be integrated into institutions in the fatherland.' We believed in the minister's word, idiots we were. 'Oh, but we didn't expect that so many would come,' De Schrijver later said and then quickly resigned… How pretentious of him! I could have killed the guy!"

"You ungrateful citizen, didn't you get your government aid every month?" Harry said snobbishly.

"Only because, legally, they couldn't do otherwise."

"At least they're doing it. That is the most important thing. I don't care to know their motivations any longer. If you know them, you'll immediately want to puke. The more you reflect on everything, the sooner you have to puke. I try to reflect on it as little as possible."

"You know what makes me puke?"

"No."

"That I saluted that rag for eleven years, every day, every morning when called."

"Rag?"

"Yeah, that rag representing Belgium."

"Ndekemopele, the great anarchist!"

"Come on! That rag. Black from the mourning mothers of soldiers, fallen in useless wars. Yellow from pus. Red from blood."

"Haha! You read too many books by Hemingway."

"Red from the blood of people like Dr. Borms. I keep seeing that image of a crippled eighty-year-old man. On crutches. Dragged to the place of execution. Shot dead like an animal by police with a black-yellow-red cockade on their damned hats, which I saluted for eleven years every morning like a damned fool."

"Ndekemopele, the great Flemish nationalist! (*starts singing the Flemish national anthem*) *They wi-i-ll not ta-a-a-me him…*"

"Quiet, Harry, let me speak. Can you still feel at home in a land where the king and cardinal shake each other's hands while there are political prisoners behind bars longing for freedom?

Can you cheer for a queen who comes from a land where the workers are still to this day extorted like medieval slaves by a bloodhound like Franco? Can you still breathe in a country where most people have snot instead of brains in their heads, whose intelligence is injected into them by TV and cheap magazines? With their endless drivel about comfort, money, TVs, cars, vacations in the Costa Brava, the Côte d'Azur, soccer during the winter, and bar chatter, and money, money, money."

"Have a Coke, you're starting to talk a lot of hot air."

"We live in a small, rotten, corrupt country where politics, unions, police, army, justice, and business form one big corrupt litter box in which I would prefer to spit!"

"You seem to have gotten something from your nice boss during those four months. I will also try to rent myself out for six thousand a month. Then I at least will learn something."

"Do you know what we all were?" said Bob, bending over the table, looking Harry right in the face.

"No."

"Servants of a system. Screwing the blacks. Servers of injustice, the trusts, Western imperialism. Hiding ourselves behind words such as Civilization, Progress, Truth, Human Rights, True Faith – beautiful masks hiding greed and hunger for power. We collaborated with an almighty white reign of terror that was convinced it was right everywhere and at all times. Which did its thing for centuries, unpunished, and – I spit on it – brought Civilization to backward people, and Truth – I vomit on it – to the dark pagan realms. They used the good old method: First, swords slashed the throats, and then crosses were left on the souls. The time of reckoning has come. Finally. Terrible for us because *we* carry the guilt. We will pay because we were the last ones left. That's the way it always is. Our skin is white and, therefore, we will pay. It is only a matter of skin color. Although U Thant and Ralph Bunche and others would pay millions to have white skin. They are wildly jealous. In the end, jealousy is all there is. So, we must not expect forgiveness. Did we ourselves show any mercy when it came down to it? Although we always talked about Mercy."

"Last week I happened to read something by that black man called Richard Wright, *White Man, Listen!* A beautiful book. A terrible book. Now suddenly it has all become very clear to me. Now I understand a lot. As a colonizer, you quickly became like the S.S. were for the Nazis. Blindly obedient. *Befehl ist Befehl*! Irrational. Merciless. Robot-like. A little bit like Eichmann. We were potential Eichmanns. How awful!"

"While you were there, you didn't realize that. Here, you do. In life, you always need slaps in the face to get to the truth. Much has become clear for me. And I reflect on it a lot. Too much."

"You're driving," Harry said.

"Go ahead and say what you think."

"First you're driving about a beautiful country, a great country, a young country where you can breathe, where you can accomplish great things, it satisfied you, etc. The next minute you start ranting about everything and more – the Belgian rag, the king, Franco, the cardinal, TV, the Côte d'Azur. Why not also get started on moral decline, marijuana smoking or the short skirts of our girls, eh, Savonarola?"

"You're avoiding my question. Didn't you have the Congo in your blood?"

"Bah," Harry said, "you shouldn't exaggerate. Everything considered, I didn't have a bad time in the Congo. I learned a lot from it. I became a man there. That is very important. It is the kind of experience that leaves a mark for life. It could have been better, but it wasn't bad. Only at the end, yeah, then…"

Bob was silent. He looked nervous and tired. He carefully shifted the remaining tangle of hair on his head.

Harry looked at the server who sat behind the counter staring into thin air. Behind the server, there was a mirror with a line of bottles in front of it.

Cinzano, Harry read, Dubonnnet, Martini…

Paul Brondeel

The Agony of a Nobody

Paul Brondeel (Lede 1927 – Bruges 2009) was a civil servant working for the customs service from 1955 to 1961 in the region of Coquilhatville (Mbandaka). His first two novels deal with the Congo: *Dagboek van een nacht. Kleine roman* (1967; Diary of One Night. Short Novel) and *Ik blanke kaffer* (1970; I White Negro), which was republished in 2019. Both novels are based on autobiographical experience.

The subtitle of *Ik blanke kaffer* is "Het verhaal van een vervreemding" (The Story of an Alienation). The title and subtitle indicate that the Congo is not a paradise. The protagonist Adriaan Cafmayer went to the Congo for selfish reasons: he wanted to earn more money and have a better life than he had in Belgium. He was not driven by any ideals. He just tried to survive as best he could. The feeling of alienation he experienced in the Congo is the direct continuation of his bleak life in Belgium. The only difference is that the setting is more exotic. Adriaan works as a level four clerk in the customs department and is sent to different customs posts. Throughout, Adriaan feels like a pawn – maltreated, not valued, and underpaid. He lacks self-confidence and, over time, his marriage with the beautiful Josiane disintegrates. Josiane, who, in contrast to Adriaan feels at home in the tropics, leaves him for a friend of his. Adriaan's life completely falls apart. In the Congo, Adriaan is a small cog in the colonial machinery, always at the mercy of others, a hardworking Fleming with a big sense of responsibility and justice. The Congo has no particular relevance to him. Adriaan's sense of alienation also applies to the colonial situation; he is acutely aware of the fact that, one day, all hell will break loose. The hatred of the Africans for the colonizers is palpable. He questions the right of the Belgians to colonize the Congo and to impose their civilization on the Congolese. In his opinion, colonization only serves the interests of the church and big capital.

Adriaan returns to Belgium in July 1960. The independence of the Congo and the subsequent riots passed him by as he descended into a haze of drunkenness and utter depression. The demise of Belgian colonization has no particular significance for him. The oppression suffered by the Congolese is not different from his own, which is why he considers himself to be a "white

Negro." Colonization is just one way in which the powerless are subjugated by the powerful. For Adriaan and others like him, there is no escape from this condition of powerlessness and victimization. He feels that, like the Congolese, he is the victim of life itself. *Ik blanke kaffer* is an intriguing existentialist novel about the desolation of life in a colonial context.

Extract originally published as:
Brondeel, P. *Ik blanke kaffer* (Antwerp: Standaard, 1970), 74–79. Translated with permission from Uitgeverij Vrijdag and the author's heirs.

I White Negro

After the Inspector had finished the procedure and installed his subordinate with one stripe, Adriaan P.K. Cafmayer, the lovely life continued, and I, the little mouse that I am, could crawl out of my hole, my little storage area, and go sniffing about left and right, and explore Kamina-City and Kamina-Base, and discover that there were five bars there, a *Cercle Wallon* and a Circle of Flemish Friends, a church, a brewery, a Monsignor, a Territorial Administrator with staff, a District Commissioner with staff, a hospital with staff – in short, everything. This was a military base that cost billions. I could observe that Kamina was a railway junction, a jewel in terms of organization and strategic importance, and I, the mouse, could see that Josiane got terribly bored and, therefore, asked for a house from the Territorial Administrator and received one (who could have refused her anything?) and made friends, to whom she explained, in my presence, that she had a husband but that this husband was married to his work and not to her.

So, I reacted and asked what she expected from me. She was disappointed, she said; she had thought…

What had she thought then? How had she imagined the Congo? As one big party, a party that would last three or four years? Full of trips, watching the wild animals, watching black people, dancing with the Watutsi, making journeys on the river, enjoying the sun and the pure air, smiling at the clouds, clapping her hands with joy, dancing, singing, balls and parties, letting the Negroes do the work, watching the Negroes lie on the ground full of awe for the white supermen, making tons of money, flirting, dating handsome men?

What had you imagined, Josiane, my dear wife? That the Congo was the land of milk and honey, where the fried chickens and *moambe* would fall in your mouth? Where the bananas and lemons and oranges could be picked from the trees? No, you didn't imagine that, but you had imagined something different from me, your husband, didn't you? That he would enjoy the evenings and nights with you instead of having to stay until ten or eleven at night to find the missing thousand francs in the accounts of the customs office, instead of curbing the chicken deliverers at Truls or fighting drunken fishermen at the border. That we would have gone hiking in the bush, travelling in the savannah, affection, love, a child, a family, instead of my eternal constraint, my restlessness, my ruminating, my years and years of alienation from everything and everyone.

We didn't have a family, our family life was dead; after four years, the exasperation had reached the point where all attempts failed, that a gap had developed, but, in spite of everything, I still loved Josiane, and I didn't want to lose her. Anna Boits or Emma Rekelman didn't matter to me at all, nor did any black bombshell with perky breasts and velvety hands, but often I felt, even with Josiane, like a stranger, a stranger who every evening rang the bell and asked to be let inside. In the same way, I felt like a stranger in this inhospitable country under the flaming sun, in my work and personal life that I never enjoyed, among people I couldn't appreciate, with Africans I could never speak to.

I had work that completely exhausted me, while elsewhere (far away, eight thousand kilometers away) they said, wrote, and screamed that every white man in Africa was a lazy fool and was totally distraught. A job that was hopeless and discouraging. It caused nothing but resentment and enmity, opposition, and suspicion. It made me neglect my family and deprived me of my friends.

Maybe I wasn't made for the Congo; too many scruples, too honest, drilled too much and too well in caring about duty and responsibility and justice. Maybe. On top of this, in this land of heat and unrest, I also had to deal with my persistent worries and reflections on the reasons for my presence there, my presence and that of all the others. I had to deal ever more with my questions about justice, honesty, the necessity of a civilizing mission, the necessity of this sublimated servitude of fifteen million natives. And then I consoled myself with at least one thing, namely that I did it for the money and that I was convinced that the rest was humbug, sublimation, and puffed up words.

And then again there were days – I had got it together and was better after a couple of months, I'd gotten myself recognized and rationalized it all to myself again – then there were days when I cried along with the choir of wolves. That meant that I was also going to the parties – attendance by that damned customs officer was, after all, expected – with Josiane, in the bloom of her youth, as pretty as heaven. I went to the party of the Walloon Circle and to that of the Flemish Friends Circle. There I could drink for free in the bar and eat the roasted suckling piglets and slowly dance the tango with Ms. Schubbe, the wife of the bar owner, cheek to cheek. I could caress her on her bare wet back, and rock to soft music, in the half-dark, dreamy eyed, a little tipsy, feeling full, in love, lost, as if in a dream. Josiane secretly received kisses from Mr. Schubbe, the bar owner, and on Christmas, Francine, from the Hotel de la Gare, hung around my neck and her husband around Josiane's. I, surrendering completely, and Josiane, surrendering completely, and in this way we cheated on each other once again, willfully, painfully, but Josiane seemed less jealous than I was. And on New Year's Eve it happened again (as on other occasions) and then we had a flaming row. We blamed each other for cheating, for adultery, the worse the better, and everything that came up again from the past, Anna Boits, Tiketik, Mokambo, fish, fighting, Couillonville, Peter Cnop, my bad habits. It always ended in tears, or walking away, or hitting the very dilapidated Vanguard car.

And afterwards, I was once again staring with empty eyes at all the Africans arriving by train in Kaminaville, hundreds of lanky Negro men and women, in rags and in filthy loincloths. The women went pooping in the field near the warehouse of the customs house (*hygiène publique*), and then they crawled again like animals in train cages. The salary of the boy was ten francs per day plus his *pocho*, and it was all legally regulated and enforced by conventions. Josiane paid her boy triple the official rate and still was ashamed about it, so she let him work from seven in the morning until noon, until after the dishes, and then he was free. Maybe the boy was happy with it, I don't know. But all these thoughts, all these considerations ate at me, a boring guy, during all the parties and at the required receptions at the house of the District Commissioner and that of the Territorial Administrator or elsewhere. Thinking, criticizing and revolting were not allowed – only flirting, hand-kissing, laughing, lying, appraising, inviting and forging sustainable bonds of friendship with Madame X and Mr. Z and with the whole bunch of white stars and stripes.

Then the time came to think about our departure, our discharge after four years of Katanga, and that brought some new excitement; we even forgot about our bickering because of that. The Vanguard was sold for pennies – or, rather, less than pennies because the thing had long lost its value – and the personal possessions, such as the refrigerator and washing machine, were stored in crates and placed in the customs warehouse. That indicated that we would come back, and Josiane was excited about it. It all looked very promising for the vacation that we thought would last for eight months.

Lieve Joris

In Search of the Real Congo

Lieve Joris (Neerpelt, 1953) writes travelogues based on her experiences in the Middle East, Eastern Europe and Africa. Congo is a recurring theme in her work. *Terug naar Congo* (1987; Back to the Congo) was followed by *Dans van de luipaard* (2001; Dance of the Leopard), *Het uur van de rebellen* (2006; The Rebels' Hour) and *De hoogvlaktes* (2008; The High Plains). In *Op de vleugels van de draak. Reizen tussen Afrika en China* (2013; On the Wings of the Dragon – Travelling between Africa and China), she follows African and Chinese traders who venture into each other's territory. In her latest book, *Terug naar Neerpelt* (2018; Back to Neerpelt), she returns to her native Belgium and writes the story she's travelled around during all those years.

With Joris, a new period in Belgian literature on the Congo begins. She was seven years old when the Belgian Congo obtained its independence. Having had a great-uncle who was a missionary and who always told riveting stories during his holidays in Belgium, Joris decided to go to Congo to retrace her great-uncle's footsteps. After listening to the nostalgic reminiscences of the remaining missionaries, she goes in search of the postcolonial Congo. She wants to find out how the Congolese look at their world, what they think about the social and political developments in their country.

Joris is interested in individual experience, in personal testimony. *Dans van de luipaard* paints the precarious situation in Congo right after Mobutu's demise. In this excerpt, Joris has travelled by boat from Mbandaka to Bokote and arrives in an old mission post where Rwandan refugees have gathered after having walked hundreds of miles through the equatorial forest.

> **Extract originally published as:**
> Joris, L. *Dans van de luipaard* (Amsterdam: Meulenhoff, 2001), 161–67.
> Translated with permission from the author.

Dance of the Leopard

I hear Séraphin stumbling and raging in the dark. I turn on my flashlight. It's five o'clock. "What is it?" I ask when he shows up, angry, framed by the doorway of my hut.

"I asked the captain," he sputters, "to leave at five to get to Bokote on time, but he is not even awake yet. If I had to leave at five, I would already be up at four. That's why I have always been the best at every job I've had. But these folks – never heard of professional pride." At any rate, he's wide awake. Not that much later everyone else is, too.

Around ten we arrive in Bokote. The beautiful mission church on the hill is surrounded by a waving field of grass and weeds. Hutu refugees roam around in the dim emptiness of the plundered mission, stare dully out at the courtyard, or lie asleep in empty classrooms. The pupils' benches were used for firewood by an earlier swarm of refugees. Two boys walk along with me. They say that some of the refugees headed to the village to look for food. Several people have died in the last few days; there were no body bags for them.

A field hospital is set up under an overhang because many refugees suffer from diarrhea, malaria and foot wounds, which prevents them from coming aboard. Nurses of *Doctors without Borders* (MSF, *Médecins Sans Frontières*), sitting on stools, put on plastic gloves, grab pieces of gauze with tweezers and dab them in metal containers of disinfecting solution. The wounded shuffle towards them, some on crutches. While sitting on the ground one boy lifts his foot up – his heel is one festering, pulsating wound. His face is distorted in a grimace of pain as the yellowish liquid drips and he moans softly. I force myself to look, but can't keep watching for long. The moaning, in no way corresponding to the amount of pain he has to be feeling, cuts through my soul. He has learned to be unassuming, even when it comes to his suffering. Out of the corner of my eye I see that he has an even much worse wound on the sole of his foot.

Two boys from the Red Cross use a stretcher to carry the sick who can't walk. They take away a young woman in a coma, her wandering eyes looking vacantly towards the equatorial sky. A third aid worker shouts at the refugees to hurry up. He is a hard-hearted man – I saw him in action earlier, according to the day workers he has been a commander under Mobutu. Fires are extinguished with water, meager possessions are tied into bundles, and the wretched column sets off.

I follow Séraphin to the mission office, where he gives the local personnel their pay – five dollars per day for the worker of the United Nations High Commissioner for Refugees, two dollars for his helpers, among whom is a nurse who unfortunately had neither medicine nor bandages to care for the refugees. A cassette recorder with miserable sound plays religious music, a crucifix hangs on the wall, a book by the Flemish writer Ward Ruyslinck is lying around — these constitute the only remains of the nuns who have lived here before.

The day laborers on the boat have also put on plastic gloves. Dieudonné carries the weakest refugees inside and when the Red Cross commander makes those waiting hurry up, causing a crush at the small entrance to the hold, he calls out: "*Malembe, malembe, bazali maladi.* Careful, careful, they are sick."

Since I'm the only white person here, the villagers of Bokote assume that I am the UNHCR coordinator. I am constantly accosted by people who claim to have helped the refugees and expect something in return. "We barely had anything of our own," complains an old man, "and after we gave them what we had, we're ruined." In fact, in his shabby clothes he really doesn't look better than the refugees.

As the time of our departure nears, the crowd becomes more desperate. They threaten that next time, they won't allow the refugees to leave just like that. Someone tells me that he has something to talk about with me and pulls me aside. He is a teacher and has helped different people but has received nothing – meanwhile, he has seen that the UNHCR worker and the nurses… Séraphin's voice turns tough when he hears those words. "Did anyone ask you to take care of the refugees? No, right? You did it out of solidarity, African solidarity" – here he looks askance at me – "something which Europeans know nothing about any longer. And now you are whining for money!"

"On the radio it was announced that we had to assist the refugees," the teacher says. "If we don't receive anything, we won't do that any longer."

"In Mbandaka we started paying people," Séraphin replies, "and you know what they did? They started to steal refugees from the camp and promised them a *chikwangue* if they pretended they had been brought by them." He sniffs disdainfully. "So we stopped doing that."

"But we just want… a piece of soap or something." Séraphin, annoyed, shakes the teacher off and pulls me along. But the man keeps running after us and talking to me. "Why don't you give me your address – then I can write you, and your journey here would have at least have produced some result."

Meanwhile all the refugees have come on board. On the beach, one Red Cross worker burns the clothes, plastic water bottles, and the UNHCR sheets that have been left behind. Another one disposes of the dirty gauze pads in the water, empties the metal trays with disinfectant solution, and rinses them. I look with a little disgust as the river water turns sort of red-yellow. Couldn't he have done that somewhere else, out of our sight?

Then we are ready to leave. The villagers of Bokote remain behind, still grumbling, but ready to wave goodbye so as not to spoil the farewell for the refugees – the strongest of them are leaning over the railing of the ship.

Séraphin stands on the deck with a cardboard box at his feet. As we leave, he throws brown pieces of *Miko* soap into the crowd. The way he stands there with feet apart, lavishly scattering the soap, makes me suspect that he has done this before, and that his display of surliness on the quay was just meant as a Séraphin-style reprimand.

The teacher is there again, waving exuberantly with two pieces of soap. "Why won't you write to me?" he shouts. All the villagers laugh at his suggestion and there is also laughter on deck, so he finds the courage to shout: "Why can't a white woman love a black man?" The villagers nudge him, clap, and slap him on the shoulder – his words get lost in a cloud of cheers. I suddenly become acutely aware of the isolation the man sinks into now that the refugees – his connection, however brief, with the outside world – are leaving. Above the shouts his lonely farewell resounds: "Why couldn't *you* love me?"

A man stands up. He moves in the direction of the toilet, a gray shadow on fragile legs. He maneuvers himself with some difficulty between the bodies closely packed against one another, but bumps against a painful leg, a wound just tended to. He is already well on his way when someone calls him back. A weak person like him cannot remain upright in the door-less room with the hole – only the strong can make it to the toilet.

He stands there, lost; a rope around his thin waist holding up pants that are many sizes too large. What now? Some know already, and chuckling spreads all around. A plastic bucket makes its way in his direction, he sees it coming – at first without understanding, then with sorrowful eyes. He takes the bucket, sets it down, and looks around. Again, there is some suppressed laughter. Hesitantly, he fiddles with the rope around his waist, lets his pants fall and squats over the bucket.

Is this a human being, who in the entryway of death still has to undergo such humiliations?

I stand on the pirogue among the nurses who distribute health booklets and medicine to the one hundred and thirty anguished people crammed together into the ship and I see scenes from the concentration camp of Primo Levi flash before me. Children with bags under their eyes, most with faces swollen from edema, gnaw on cardboard-colored biscuits. Everyone has an itch, everyone is scratching – all except the woman in a coma, who seems to have left behind the forest of horrors they have all emerged from.

To think that all these people once had worthiness and dignity, a house, a piece of land on a hill. Before they… because that is what is confusing: they are not just victims, some have taken part in a crime that is in the meantime seen as almost a collective crime. They have become like the Serbs; they have blood on their hands. The further inland they traveled in the Congo, the guiltier they were considered. Why else keep on fleeing? Why didn't they go home if they had nothing to reproach themselves for?

But if the unfortunate people who sit together under the rusty ceiling have in fact killed, hasn't the odyssey they have experienced and from which they have emerged as almost half human – hasn't that somehow purified them? Haven't they been punished enough?

Some are in better shape than others. They have lived for a while with the Congolese, according to the nurses, they had a chance to recover. And then there are those who seem remarkably healthy, probably soldiers from the former Rwandan government forces, who had the refugees work for them along the way. Their eyes have a hardened look, and they possess strength the others have lost from suffering hunger and neglect. Their feet show no wounds or sores because they have worn military boots the whole time. One blanket is distributed for every five refugees, but the next morning I see a soldier comfortably wrapped up in a whole blanket.

A commotion arises in the front part of the ship. A girl who has been in a comatose state and who had been tossing and turning with a painful expression on her face, is becoming increasingly agitated. In her delirium she moves her head back and forth, suffers convulsions with her arms, and strikes out with her legs as if she wanted to kick the pain out of her body. Those nearby try to avoid her movements, draw their feet away, and look to the helpers beseechingly. Félicien, the youngest MSF nurse, looks towards her.

"Cerebral malaria," he says.

"Can't you do anything?"

"No, in Mbandaka maybe, but not here."

The tough Red Cross commander behind us taps Félicien on the shoulder "Step aside, please."

Irritated, Félicien turns around: "Can't you see I'm busy?"

The commander gives him an angry push and before I know it they are going at one another. Félicien is much weaker than his opponent so he almost falls in the water. Startled, I pull them apart. The commander's eyes shoot fire. "That guy there from MSF… what is he thinking!" His colleagues try to calm him down, and Félicien also gets calming pats on the shoulder. The refugees look on with resignation. Have they already been witnesses to such scenes, or have they become indifferent to the tumult that comes from the land of the living?

Like a wounded animal, Félicien later licks his wounds. "The Red Cross should not think it is better than MSF," he says, "especially not that commander of Mobutu." He looks at me with fear in his eyes. "You know that he intended to toss me in the water? That's what he told his friends." I try to comfort him but I'm also shocked by what happened. Their lack of unity while surrounded by people who are mortally ill surprises me. If they can't put aside their personal conflicts in difficult circumstances like these, how will they ever work together and – rebuild their country, for example? Mobutu has gone, but the disunity he has sowed among his people has remained.

I think of all this while I sit on the deck with Félicien, my arm on his shoulder. Séraphin looks down at us with a mocking grin. "How's it going?" Word of the incident spread throughout the ship, so he naturally knows all about it. Félicien gets up, rubs his eyes, casts a furtive glance over the railing, clenches his teeth and heads downstairs.

Markus Leroy

Political Games

Markus Leroy (Deinze 1946) studied geography and development cooperation. For thirty-five years, he held leading administrative positions in the Belgian Department of Development Aid. From 1985 to 1991, he worked in this capacity at the Belgian embassy in Kinshasa. He also worked in a number of other African countries. He wrote *Afrika retour* (1993; Africa Retour), *Hendana* (1995), which is set in Burundi, and *Gekleurd, in zwart-wit* (1999; Colored, in Black and White).

In *Afrika retour*, the main character heads the Belgian Development Aid Service in a country that is not named but is easily recognizable as the Congo (or Zaïre, as it was known under President Joseph Désiré Mobutu). As a result of the corruption of the Congolese government and the politicization of the Belgian Department of Development Aid, no efficient assistance is possible. Only a cynical attitude allows the main character to function in such an environment. The title of the book may be taken to refer both to the demise of Africa and to the fact that the main character is on his way back to Belgium after only one year at his post in Kinshasa.

The novel sketches a number of incidents, including a visit to a development project in the jungle, a visit to the presidential palace in the interior, and even an abduction by dissatisfied aid workers. These incidents suggest that development aid makes no sense and that every human being is first and foremost motivated by self-interest. The main character can only ascertain the bankruptcy of a country and of development aid: "He understood less and less what kind of sense it made to pump millions into this country each year … but he realized that the people around the table would not appreciate such an attitude from someone in his position. It made no sense, he thought, to endanger his job by saying things his superiors preferred not to hear. Life here was not bad at all, and he rather wanted to enjoy it for a little bit longer." One year later, the African president stops all Belgian development projects, and the main character has to return to Belgium, convinced that development aid is useless. *Afrika retour* is a disturbing novel that radically dismisses the postcolonial era of guilt and penance.

Extract originally published as:
Leroy, M. *Afrika retour* (Leuven: Davidsfonds, 1993), 132–37.
Translated with permission from Standaard Uitgeverij.

— Africa Retour

"That's what the company took care of," the project leader said without hesitating. He didn't seem to have a problem with it. "Just as that company also takes care of our housing. And not so badly, as you may have noticed," he added proudly.

They visited a wide-open field; on one side, workers were busy chopping trees and branches to pieces with chainsaws. Those were taken away by truck, and, further up where all the wood was gone, a tractor was ploughing. There new palm trees would be planted soon. Elsewhere, a plow with the same sort of saw was taking away the undergrowth from the old plantations. They also visited the artificial fertilizer distribution center that had only recently been opened because it took more than a year for the fertilizers to arrive from the distributor in Europe. In another place, they saw a nursery for young palm oil trees: some trees only had one small green leaf above the ground, others were ready to be uprooted. It all looked very professional and well-organized.

Later in the afternoon when the site visit was over, they went outside to drink on the terrace of the guest house. You could still smell the old colonial atmosphere there: red scrubbed cement floor, *fauteuils-morris* armchairs and a parlor table in heavy tropical wood. In front of the house, a gardener was mowing the grass with a *coupe-coupe*. The houseboy wore a stiffly ironed white cotton suit but walked barefoot. You could still feel the glorious days of the colonial past. At least for those who sat on the terrace.

"How is the cooperation with the villagers now?" asked Lodewijk. "You said earlier that they weren't interested in improving or expanding their plantations. Is it better now?"

"It is outstanding now," the project leader answered. "Many of them are employed by us. We pay them fairly, and I think that they realize that everything we're doing benefits them in the end. These are all village plantations, you know. The oil company doesn't gain anything from them directly."

That was the perfect moment for Dick to launch into a verbal attack. He had walked around the whole day with a face like a thundercloud, and now the storm broke loose.

"Are you that naïve, or is it simple complicity?" he started. "You say the oil company doesn't gain anything directly from this but, indirectly, it gains much more. They have a factory here which they haven't invested a single dime in for over thirty years. Their only costs are the salaries of the local workers and of the few foreigners. They buy the palm nuts at the lowest possible price, just enough so that the villagers won't stop supplying them. And they can do that because the people in the villages can't go anywhere else with their nuts. It's no wonder, then, that the people aren't interested in maintaining their own plantations any longer, let alone starting up new ones. And what do those smart young guys from the company do? They take a non-governmental organization (NGO) under their wing. That is very clever: NGOs are popular in Belgium because their work allegedly benefits the people directly, whereas the official development aid only seems to support a corrupt regime. One of those naive professors in tropical agriculture writes an application for them, the proposal reaches the appropriate ministry that sends it on to our department. The company deposits 25%, the project is approved, and the deal is done. The company makes the Belgian state pay for 75% of the investments, which they would never decide to do without this support. And in this way, production shortly takes off without costing them much of anything. Nice. I'd also like to do business that way."

"What a diatribe," the project leader responded. "But before I respond to that, you may want to drink something, on that clever company's dime. At least then all that money isn't wasted." The project leader ordered some beers, a popular drink here, and responded.

"You say that the company isn't investing here anymore. Sure. But who is still investing in this country? Would you invest in an enterprise that starts to pay off only in five to ten years? With all the uncertainties here? And it isn't true that the palm nuts are purchased too cheaply. In the current situation, you just can't afford to pay more. You have no idea what it costs to get the processed oil transported to the seaport, over these roads or on the totally unreliable ships on the river. If the company didn't maintain the roads here in the area, no one would do it, and everything would just stop. So it is simply not true that they don't have costs other than salaries and the purchase of palm nuts."

"So they stay here out of philanthropic conviction," Dick interrupted.

"I'm not saying that, but, in my opinion, they're not making unreasonable profits. If they are making profits at all in the current situation."

"Do you have numbers to back that up? Have you ever seen their actual accounts? And I don't mean the numbers they publish for the public."

"No, but I am convinced it is true. I also have to say something about the project itself. Mechanization is the only way to modernize African agriculture. Can you imagine if all the work you saw this afternoon had to happen by hand? That has simply become unthinkable. The people don't want to do that anymore. If you want to keep the African farmer in the countryside, you have to help him modernize local agriculture. Otherwise, they'll all leave for the city."

"But have you ever calculated what that costs?" Dick asked again. "I mean, if the whole project has to be paid with the profit from palm oil, is it profitable then?"

"In the short term certainly not. You must consider this a test-project that in itself can't be profitable. But if the general situation in the country should improve – the roads, the waterways, the ports – if the entire governmental organization was better and less corrupt, then it should become profitable."

"In a thousand years, when gold nuggets grow on the palm trees."

"Yes, I know. But tell me what is profitable in this country? Should we then give up agriculture altogether?"

"Food production has to be profitable," Dick said, "if they at least didn't import all that subsidized stuff. It is always the same: we are trying to use our foreign aid to build up what we ourselves had earlier helped to destroy. And we'd rather give them food aid then teach them how to produce it themselves."

Lodewijk listened attentively but didn't say anything. It occurred to him that wherever people engaged in developmental aid, they devoted a large part of their time and energy to discussions on what should happen and how or whether it all made any sense. Entire libraries were already filled with such discussions, but they continued without ever coming to a conclusion. The funniest thing was that only the donors were talking about it. The recipients of the help barely had a chance to say anything. Did they not have any opinion on how things should be organized in their country? Lodewijk had already formed his opinion that only cynicism could keep you in this country. It therefore seemed better to him not to take part in a discussion between people who still believed in the benefits of foreign aid.

The discussion went on for some time. Dick still did not agree with the vision of the volunteers, but, with the setting of the sun, the talks became less biting and gradually transitioned to less controversial topics, such as the quality of the different brands of terrain vehicles, always a fascinating topic for anyone who had to work in the African bush. They all agreed that the Japanese had gotten ahead of the Americans and the Europeans, especially the English with their antiquated Land Rovers.

That evening, all of them were invited, visitors and volunteers, to a dinner at the house of the factory director. He lived in a big mansion with a very young black woman, whom he introduced as his mistress without hesitation. "For years, my wife hasn't been able to live here," he later explained, "and so I sought some company." The woman stuck to his side and served him the whole evening like a slave. And when they went on to the parlor after the meal, she sat like a well-behaved pet on the rug at his feet.

A couple of times, Dick tried to resume the discussion on the project, but the director warded off his attacks handily by dishing up one fascinating story after another. Was he scared of confrontation, or had he given up caring about development in Africa, let alone having flaming conversations about it?

The following day was the last and also the longest day of the whole trip. They wanted to drive back to the capital in one day. It was around six hundred kilometers, the first two hundred of which were over sand and the rest over the same bad asphalt they had experienced on the first day. They prepared everything the evening before and left in the morning around five o'clock. The African weather gods were in their favor that day, and they didn't need to use any ferry-bridges. They made good progress – in African terms, that is.

However exhausting the route, this was the way back, and the longing for "home" made it all seem not quite so bad. Sometime before ten o'clock at night, they drove into the capital and Lodewijk noted that, of the six days, they had spent four on the road and hardly had two for visiting. "That doesn't seem very efficient to me," he said, "but maybe that explains why this country can't develop."

List of References

Anbeek, T. "Het donkere hart. Walschap, Geeraerts en de Kongo," *Ons Erfdeel*: jg. 38 nr. 1 (1995).

Bergeyck, J. *Het onweer*, in: *Verhalen uit Kongo* (Brecht: De Roerdomp, 1988).

Bittremieux, L. *Mayombsche penneschetsen* (Bruges: Sint Michiel, 1914)

Bossaerts, H. *Herinneringen aan Congo. Désiré Bossaerts ambtenaar in Boma (1904–1907)* (Antwerp: Manteau, 2007).

Brondeel, P. *Ik blanke kaffer* (Antwerp: Standaard, 1970).

Buysse, C. *De zwarte kost* (1889), in: *Verzameld werk 4* (Brussels: Manteau, 1974).

Danco, P. *Ook een ideaal* (Ghent: A. Siffer, 1896).

De Deken, C. *Twee jaren in Congoland* (1902), in: *Twee Jaar in Congo* (Antwerp: De Vlijt, 1952).

De Jonghe, S. *Het koloniale in de literatuur* (Turnhout: Van Mierlo-Proost, 1938).

De Mey, P. *Van Antwerpen naar Stanley-Pool* (Turnhout: Joseph Splichal, 1899).

De Moor, P. "Terug naar Kongo van Heeroom: Interview met Lieve Joris," *HN Magazine*: 25 April 1987.

De Sadeleer, R. *Palaver om de ebbe* (Antwerp: Boekengilde Die Poorte, 1960).

Foeken, D. *"België behoeft een kolonie". De ontstaansgeschiedenis van Kongo Vrijstaat* (Antwerp/Amsterdam: De Vries en Brouwers, 1985).

Geeraerts, J. *Schroot* (1963), 2ᵉ ed. (Antwerp: Manteau, 1990).

Joris, L. *Dans van de luipaard* (Amsterdam: Meulenhoff, 2001).

Leroy, M. *Afrika retour* (Leuven: Davidsfonds, 1993).

Nacht, B. *De kerstnacht van Baliongo* (1949), in: *Kongo ya lobi* (Leuven: Davidsfonds, 1961).

Poortmans, R. *Moeder, ik sterf* (The Hague: Servire, 1932).

Schoup, J. *Blanke boeien* (Velsen: Schuyt, 1934).

Tilemans, E. *Bendsjé of de liefde der negerin* (Brussels: A. Lambrechts, 1931).

Van Aken, P. *De nikkers* (1959), 6ᵉ ed. (Antwerp: Houtekiet, 2001).

Van Booven, H. *Tropenwee* (1904), in: *Amsterdam: Maatschappij voor goede en goedkoope lectuur* (s.a.).

Van den Weghe, J. *De inlandse schoolmeester* (1965), in: *Kinderen van Kongo* (Brussels: Manteau, 1965).

Van der Cruyssen, A-C. *Afrika, naar de beste bronnen* (Kortrijk: Ch. Vandesteene, 1877).

Ver Boven, D. *De rode aarde die aan onze harten kleeft* (Brussels: Reinaert, 1962).

Verreet, A. *Het zwarte leven van Mabumba* (Leuven: Davidsfonds, 1935).

Walschap, A. *Longwangu de smid*, in: *Het letterkundig werk van Alfons Walschap*, intr. Vital Celen (Antwerp: De Sikkel, 1952).

Walschap, G. *Oproer in Congo* (Amsterdam: Elsevier, 1953).

CPSIA information can be obtained
at www.ICGtesting.com
Printed in the USA
LVHW012242270620
659204LV00004B/46